Advance Praise

"**Kevin Curtis** has written a masterpiece for educators at all levels. *The Connection-Driven Classroom: Proactive and Practical Tools to Improve Student Behaviors* focuses on the most significant vehicle to learning relationships. His connection-driven focus is much needed in the twenty-first-century classroom, and I am therefore certain that countless educators will find the contents of this book to be most beneficial to learning in their schools and classrooms."
   —**Baruti Kafele**, retired principal, education consultant, author

"For years, educators have been told, 'The deeper the relationship, the deeper the learning.' Finally, the best in the business has provided us with a manual for exactly *how* to do just that. When it comes to providing teachers with the blueprint, strategy, tools, and step-by-step instructions for connecting with kids so we can more effectively deliver our content, no one is better than **Kevin Curtis**."
   —**Hal Bowman**, coauthor of *Dear Teacher: 100 Days of Inspirational Quotes and Anecdotes* and host of the Teach Like a Rock Star podcast

"**Kevin Curtis** has done transformational work as a professional educator and trained thousands of others in how to create dynamic, welcoming, and inclusive spaces where all students feel connected. This is a must-read for all educational practitioners. You'll be inspired, empowered, and equipped."
   —**James Whitfield**, EdD, award-winning educator

"**Kevin Curtis** has shown time and time again that relationships are the foundation of our educational system. In his book, *The Connection-Driven Classroom*, he has taken this philosophy and shared practical strategies to elevate the health, connection, and ultimately achievement of the students we serve."
    —**Kate Barker**, speaker, coach, retired principal, and coauthor of
    Principaled: Navigating the Leadership Learning Curve

"**Kevin Curtis** is dedicated to doing what's right for students and educators alike, listening to the voices of those he serves to transform the educational experience for all. He knows that real change in the classroom starts by connecting with the heart and discovering the passions and potential in every student. This book is essential for educators who want to deepen their impact, foster meaningful connections, and ultimately equip the destinies of the students they teach."
    —**Dave Schmittou**, EdD, former professor, principal, assistant
    principal, coach, and teacher

"This groundbreaking book provides an invaluable toolkit for fostering authentic, trust-based relationships in educational and organizational settings. By focusing on honest communication and collective meaning, it offers practical strategies for enhancing classroom engagement, saving time, and building empowered, value-driven connections. With insights on persistence and the importance of being seen and heard, this resource is essential for educators and leaders committed to nurturing a positive, impactful environment where every student and team member is truly valued."
    —**Frankie Mendoza**, School District Coordinator of
    Restorative Practices

"**Kevin Curtis** has created a guide for educators who want to create meaningful and lasting relationships with their students. He lays out proactive and practical tools designed to improve student behaviors by focusing on connections rather than punishment. Through engaging strategies like the 'Meet & Greet' and the '60-Second Relate Break,' Kevin offers a step-by-step guide to fostering an inclusive and supportive classroom environment where students feel valued, seen, and heard."

—Adam Dovico, EdD, professor, former principal,
author, presenter

"The most fundamental unit of energy in all classrooms is the moment of genuine connection. Creating these on a regular basis with every student on my roster continues to be one of the most important things I do as a teacher. These moments look deceptively simple, but what **Kevin Curtis** will teach you in this book is that they are carefully, intentionally, and skillfully created. He'll show you how to get there — keep reading."

—Dave Stuart
Author of The Will to Learn and These Six Things

"*The Connection-Driven Classroom* highlights not only the importance of building relationships with students, but also provides clear guidance on how to do it. **Kevin Curtis** offers a practical blueprint for creating a supportive, inclusive classroom where every student feels valued and understood—it's a toolkit every teacher needs!"

—Kim Strobel, author of Teach Happy: Small Steps to Big Joy,
speaker, and owner of Strobel Education

"As a former superintendent, I find *The Connection-Driven Classroom* a valuable resource for both individual educators and entire school districts. **Kevin Curtis** offers practical, easy-to-implement tools that help build strong teacher-student relationships while also providing a scalable framework to transform school culture. This book is essential for any district looking to improve student engagement, reduce disciplinary issues, and foster a positive, supportive learning environment. Curtis's connection-driven approach can potentially transform individual classrooms and entire schools, setting the foundation for long-term success in any educational setting."

—Chris Galloway, Executive Coach / Former Superintendent

"*The Connection-Driven Classroom* by **Kevin Curtis** focuses on the importance of building strong, positive relationships between students and teachers to enhance educational outcomes. You will find practical strategies for teachers to connect with their students, fostering a classroom environment that is conducive to learning through caring and supportive relationships. Key points include everyday techniques and tools for developing meaningful interactions, the benefits of a connected classroom on student learning and behavior, and methods for teachers to cultivate a nurturing and inclusive atmosphere. Overall, the book serves as a guide for educators to create a classroom culture around connection and mutual respect, which ultimately drives student success and well-being."

—**Jim Sporleder**, National School Trauma Informed Trainer

"**Kevin Curtis** has revolutionized the way we educate, grow, and simply 'do' school with our students. He has been a shining light for stakeholders within the school system from teachers to students to administrators. His practices have made him the guru on the establishment...In this book, Kevin not only gives schools the *why* but he also can provide the tools on *how.*"

–**Ryan Brassel**, Assistant Principal, Northside Independent School District

"I highly recommend *The Connection-Driven Classroom.* This insightful book highlights the crucial difference between making connections and building relationships in the classroom, providing practical strategies that empower teachers to create meaningful interactions with their students. The emphasis on intentionality in fostering connections is essential for improving student behavior and enhancing classroom dynamics. A must-read for any educator looking to make a lasting impact!"

—**Dr. Brad Johnson**, Educational Leader, Inspirational Speaker, and Author

The
Connection-Driven Classroom
Proactive and Practical Tools to Improve Student Behaviors

Kevin Curtis

Ⓓ **Differentiated Discipline**

The Connection-Driven Classroom:
Proactive and Practical Tools to Improve Student Behaviors
© copyright 2024
Kevin Curtis

Ⓓ Differentiated Discipline

ISBN ebook: 978-1-964014-40-1
ISBN paperback: 978-1-964014-41-8
ISBN hardcover: 978-1-964014-42-5

Library of Congress Control Number 2024918640.

Published by Tasfil Publishing, LLC
Voorhees, New Jersey

Table of Contents

Introduction: The Currency of Connections 1

Part I: The Story of CDC and its TCT 17

1. A Little (More) about Me....................................19

2. Relationships vs. Connections 37

3. What Makes a Teacher Outstanding?....................47

Part II: TCT for Schools 69

Caveat: 71

4. Tool #1: The Meet & Greet................................79

5. Tool #2: The 60-Second Relate Break 89

6. Tool #3: The 2-Minute Connection 97

7. Tool #4: The Positive Spark 117

8. Tool #5: The Treatment Agreement....................135

9. GTKY Questions 161

Conclusion: Believe 169

Acknowledgments 177

About the Author..179

Dedication

To all the educators who have made a difference in the lives of their students, this book is dedicated to you. Your tireless dedication, unwavering commitment, and selfless service have shaped the lives of countless individuals, including mine. You have taught us not only academic subjects but also life lessons that will stay with us forever.

You have inspired us to dream big, to aim high, and to never give up on ourselves. You have believed in us even when we didn't believe in ourselves, and you have pushed us to be the best versions of ourselves. You have nurtured our talents and abilities and helped us discover our passions and interests.

You have been our mentors, our role models, and our guides, showing us the way when we were lost and cheering us on when we succeeded. You have listened to us, cared for us, and supported us, both inside and outside the classroom.

Your impact on our lives cannot be measured by grades, awards, or accolades but by the way we live our lives, the choices we make, and the people we become. You have left an indelible mark on our hearts and minds, and we will forever be grateful for your guidance and influence.

So to all the educators who have touched our lives in ways big and small, thank you. Thank you for inspiring us, for believing in us, and for making us who we are today. May your legacy continue to live on through the generations of students whose lives you have touched.

Introduction

The Currency of Connections

I define connection as the energy that exists between people when they feel seen, heard, and valued. When they can give it, when they can receive, when they can give and receive without judgment. And when they derive sustenance and strength from the relationship.
—Brené Brown[1]

My cat, Kai, likes to post himself near my computer while I write. I'm probably not the only one whose cat's big mission in life is to obstruct work. He'll sit in my lap, stand right in front of my monitor, or even walk on my keyboard. Sometimes, he'll hold his tail under my nose, giving me a big furry mustache like I'm Sam Elliott about to ride the range. It's hard not to lose concentration and laugh, give a pet, or bat him away in exasperation. It's no great mystery why he does this. He just wants what everyone wants: to be valued, seen, and heard. To feel connected. To say, "I am here!" and be acknowledged by the people he looks up to.

In other words, Kai acts a lot like our students, something I'm reminded of each time I step into a classroom, as happened recently, when I was working with a sixth-grade class. I was there consulting on how to build relationships in the classroom. That's my main job now, consulting. After the initial workshops, about once a month, I'd go back to see how the educators were doing with

---

[1] https://www.oprah.com/own-super-soul-sunday/excerpt-the-gifts-of-imperfection-by-dr-brene-brown/5

1

the tools they were learning. Always, I'd discover the energy we created was contagious.

That day, a seventh-grade teacher stopped me. "Hey, I know I haven't officially been trained in your techniques, but I've heard a lot about them from other educators. The next time you come, if you have an open period, I'd love it if you'd visit my class and show me and my students what some of these relationship tools look like."

On my return, I met with the seventh-grade teacher's class. This was my first time with them. I walked in with my trusty backpack, and I guess my reputation preceded me because all the students started exclaiming, "It's Circle Guy!" (At the time, I was doing relational activities in circles.)

"What questions are you going to ask us?"

"Watch out; he's gonna make you talk about your mom!"

"Watch out; he's gonna make you cry!"

These may have been childish taunts, but I immediately recognized these students saw me as more therapist than educator, and they didn't trust me. Recognition of a lack of a relationship is a valuable lesson. Their perception of me may have been wrong, but it was their reality, and instead of invalidating it, I had to hear it, see it, and start there. I knew they would resist responding to me directly, so I had to go an indirect route and take the pressure off.

"My name is Mr. Curtis. Some people call me the Circle Guy. But you know what? Today is not even going to be about circles. It's just a chance to get to know each other. So we're going to do a couple rounds of an activity that I think will be really fun. And I'm not going to put a question on the board. I'm going to use my conversation cubes, and we're going to let the dice roll!"

From my backpack, I pulled out a handful of premade conversation cubes I'd bought on Amazon. Each side had a Get to Know You (GTKY) question or conversation-starter written on it. We got into our circle, and I set the ground rules: "We want everyone to feel heard, so let's not talk over each other. We want everyone to feel seen, so let's look at each other's faces."

"Okay, Mr. Curtis!" the class agreed.

I passed out the cubes so everyone could look at them. "The cubes are our talking pieces. Whatever question we roll, we answer.

Can I get a thumbs-up ? "

No thumbs-up.

Well, do or die. I would model the first connection. I rolled the cube, held it, and picked it up as my talking piece. "If you could be any kind of cereal, what would you be? That's easy: Cocoa Puffs."

I handed my cube off to the student on the right, and the game was on. Pretty soon, the classroom looked like a casino. Cubes were rolling around the space, and students were squealing, "What is it? What is it?" as they waited to see what question they got. Students scrambled after the cubes and raised their hands in victory when they settled. They asked to go out of order, and I let them. They even made up their own rules: "If it rolls in front of you, you have to answer it!" It was a bit off script, but it was fun. And all of a sudden, everyone was excited about having conversations and sharing.

Then a conversation cube rolled out of the excitement, and one student picked it up. "Oh, man. I thought you said we weren't gonna have to talk about these things."

I looked at him, not sure which question he was staring at. These were supposed to be shallow, fun questions; there shouldn't have been any that inspired such a look of trepidation.

I reassured the student, "At the end of the day, I want you to feel comfortable. I want you to feel valued, seen, and heard. If we need to reroll the dice, we reroll."

He looked at the cube again. "No, I'll answer it: when my parents got divorced." Then he handed off the cube to the next student, and it went around again.

The prompt he got? "A time when you were sad."

Your question starts the conversation.
Your response shapes the conversation.

The space we create in a moment of connection is like a swimming pool: it has a shallow and a deep end. Like these simple, prefab cubes, the tools in this book are designed to stay at the shallow end. We are not therapists, after all. But a little bit of connection and trust—making that pool a safe place with us as lifeguards—can sometimes encourage a student to go deep. And sometimes it takes only minutes.

It's okay if students go deep. It's a sign they feel safe and the relationship is healthy. We don't have to fix it; we don't have to probe at it. We have to value, see, and hear the connection that is offered. That's all they need from us.

Trevor Taylor, former language arts teacher at Karen Wagner High School in the Judson Independent School District in Converse, Texas, visited my podcast once.[2] When talking about the educator's role in connecting with students, he explained it like this: "Every time a student walks into the classroom, they're waiting on the adult to make the first move. They want to see where you're taking them. If you take that first step in connecting with them. They will typically step towards you. How you respond is how they'll respond, so you have to lead."

Sometimes that leadership is asking for support. I'm thankful for the seventh-grade teacher who asked me to be part of her class, especially since she went out of her lane to do it. She was willing to try something not even assigned to her because it looked like it would help. She got vulnerable. She opened her classroom door to the Circle Guy, the guy who made students cry.

And I'm thankful for the student who showed his own vulnerability and trust by answering that question honestly. His leadership modeled to his peers that adults are to be trusted with deeply personal information and that it is worth extending an olive branch if it can make a connection.

This story shows just how little time it can take to create a connection as long as you are genuine, intentional, and compassionate. Sometimes, it can take years for a student to go deep. Sometimes not at all. That's okay too. As educators, we're not

---

[2] Both podcasts can be found here:
https://www.listennotes.com/podcasts/relationship-centered-learning-kevin-curtis-bLgmK_7Gkqu/

looking for them to jump into the deep end; we just want them to get in the pool. As long as the offer to share is on the table and the choice is given to go shallow or deep, students will respond to and appreciate our effort.

There is currency in the connections. The student responses are so valuable. Even simple questions like "What is your favorite thing to drink in the morning?" will pay off. Let's say a student responds to it with "An energy drink, like Prime." How does that response hold any value? Perhaps, three weeks after you heard this simple, shallow answer, the student comes into class seeming down. Reading their energy and body language, you know something is off.

You instinctually ask, "Did you have your Prime this morning?"

With a puzzled look, the student replies, "How do you know that I drink Prime?"

With a grin, you share with him, "I remember you shared that during our 60-Second Relate Break a few weeks ago."

The student is shocked. They are thinking, *Are you a mind reader? You listened to me? You remember what I said weeks ago?*

Tell me a moment like that captured from a 60-Second Relate break isn't valuable. Your students will be more engaged and connected to you because you made them feel heard. Now that's a valuable experience!

In addition, connections create trust, which is central to relationships. If we want students to jump into the deep end of learning, they must first wade into the shallow end of connections. The best learning environments are ones centered on classroom community connections, hence The Connection-Driven Classroom (CDC) and its Teacher Connection Toolkit (TCT) that this book offers.

How Do I Know Anything about Connections?

Before we go any further, it's important that you, the reader, make a connection with me, the author. *#ConnectB4Content.* After all, I have to model the best practices I will share with you. I'm part of this learning community, too, and whether you've volunteered or been voluntold to read this book, I want us to make the best of it.

First, even though I've been an educator, I do not know what you are going through as a teacher or administrator at this time and in this place. I see you; I know the work that you're going through, but I don't know *exactly* what you're dealing with. With politics, pandemics, wars, and the seemingly endless stream of content and tests educators are expected to work into their limited time, it seems like it gets harder to be an educator every year.

So even though I'm here and you are there, I want to acknowledge that I value, see, and hear your work. I'll do my best to make the Connection-Driven Classroom (CDC) and its Teacher Connection Toolkit (TCT) in this book easy to use.

Throughout this book, you'll probably learn twenty-five facts about me. These regular points of sharing are what build our relationship as reader and author. This is how we get to know each other. Not all at once, but through in-the-moment, incremental revelations and feelings of familiarity and association that connect us—a shared past, present, and, hopefully, future.

I'm from San Antonio, Texas. If you've been to San Antonio yourself, you probably made it to the downtown Riverwalk, which is synonymous with the city. It's a lucrative tourist hot spot featuring the Alamo, restaurants, quirky shops, and, of course, bars. It was also lucrative for me. That's how I put myself through college: bartending for seven and a half years.

We can talk about margarita recipes later (and if you've lived in or visited Texas, you know the love of a good margarita down here), but I want you to notice it took me seven and a half years to finish college. Why did it take me that long? Well, I was doing cash for college, paying as I went. I didn't want to do a lot of student loans, and while my parents could and did help, they didn't have a lot of money to spare.

I also had my first child at twenty-one years old in the middle of my educational career, and that responsibility, as any of us with students can attest, takes priority. My daughter, Krystal with a K (I love K's and alliteration—in addition to my cat, Kai, I have another cat named Kira and two dogs, K'La and Kade), graduated from the University of Texas at San Antonio just like me. I consider my daughter a success, not because she's amazing and beautiful with blue hair, but because:

1. She's very successful at working multiple jobs with large corporations.
2. She recently married the man of her dreams.
3. She and her husband just closed on their first house.
4. She has built an online community on Twitch, where—I am proud to say—she innately allows her followers to feel valued, seen, and heard.
5. She keeps building connections in the family.

When I graduated from college, I became a teacher. That's my why (why I stuck with my education): I wanted to be an educator. I wanted to help students learn. And I was a good teacher and coach. Then I became a good principal and assistant principal, but not for the reasons I had hoped.

I lost my why when I realized suspension was not why I got into education.

When I was assistant principal at Ed White Middle School's Title I campus, roughly 80 percent of the students were in a minority group. Each day, I sat at my desk, a cog in a machine of a systemic problem that set my students up to fail. Once I realized my part in this system, it was hard to stay a cog. I wanted to resign.

But I didn't want my resignation to be for nothing, as another cog would be put in place. I wanted to prevent that from happening. I also wanted to be open-minded. I'd finally been forced to look at the problem: we were running the same play every time and gaining no ground. I no longer wanted to be part of a system that set our students up to fail. I wanted to help fix it.

That awareness gave me the courage to leave K–12 education, leave my comfy salary and benefits, and build a private business that taught teachers and administrators a better way to help students succeed and help manage their behaviors—a way based not on punishment and exclusion but on relationships and inclusion.

Connections Are the Cornerstone

Educators are well aware of the problem that led me to leave the school system. They live with it every day. Ask any educator, "How's the semester going?" and you'll get similar responses.

There'll be a pause, and the educator will stare vacantly past your ear, at the horizon, just for a moment. Then they will come back to you, sigh or laugh or smile, and say, "It's going." Probe a little deeper, though, and you'll find there's a world of heartbreak in that first pause.

Frustration, sorrow, confusion, even irritation—those are the emotions educators and school administrators battle on a daily basis. We go home every night, unable to let go of our students' stories and the stress of knowing they need more. What's worse, educators are at a loss as to what more to give, especially when we are already spread too thin. We are doing so many other things than teaching content, but it's content—reading, writing, arithmetic, science—that heavily drives school outcomes and evaluations.

COVID-19 exponentially increased preexisting achievement gaps, and it pushed us further away at a time we needed to be closer together. Meanwhile, our students are still asking for more from us. I have students speak at the National Educators for Restorative Practices conferences all the time. And they always say a version of the same thing. Value us, even when we don't want to be valued. See us, even when we don't want to be seen. Hear us, even when we don't want to be heard.

Value, see, and hear. Those are the core actions behind relationships.

The pandemic made the struggle to treat each other better so much harder. It made teaching content so much harder. It made us hard as we struggled, barely holding it together.

The COVID-19 pandemic didn't cause inequities and problems with relationships, but it sure pulled back the rug to expose the dirt we already knew was there and dumped a whole truckload more on top of it. While this book isn't solely about a new "pandemic pedagogy" (because many of our practices predate the pandemic), we definitely feel the heightened urgency to meet students where they're at as they return from that disruption. Specifically, students are getting back into face-to-face environments where they have to sit in a classroom and interact in physical space and time with their peers and educators. They're two grades ahead of where they started before the pandemic, but for many, "ninth grader" is just a label. They may be bigger physically, but socially, and sometimes academically, they're in a state of arrested development—they're still where they were prior to lockdown. Educators are also feeling the stress of not having the connections that keep students participating. We feel our students slipping even further away, beyond our ability to help.

The system, as I learned and as many of you sense, is already broken. As long as we keep patching and gluing the rotten and outgrown parts back together, this system still gets to pass as a good house for learning, even as its nineteenth-century foundation crumbles under the strain of modern life.

But wouldn't it be nice if we could just rebuild? Fix the system from the ground up? Keep our students by valuing, seeing, and hearing their differences?

There has to be a better way than barely holding it together.

We can't avoid these problems anymore. Teaching is becoming mentally and emotionally unsustainable, and with increasing educator loss and a shortage now exacerbated, we can't afford to let the problem go on any longer.

And schools know there's a problem. There are so many things that schools are trying to do to regain some ground on relationship-building after the pandemic. When I ask school leaders how they're doing that, they give me something like this: "We have a social-emotional software the educators use in lesson plans," or "We have cultural diversity, and we talk to students about where they're at this time." Okay, but how are you checking in on these initiatives? How do these impactful and challenging conversations happen when the students and educators don't even know each other?

School leaders constantly introduce school initiatives they feel will fix the problem of high-needs students—SEL, diversity, culture, content, character, whatever is needed to complete the whole child—but they don't think about the interpersonal dynamics that will deliver that content. New initiatives demand students and educators simultaneously build relationships and build knowledge. But these things can't be done at the same time, especially when the accountability and how-to of building relationships are so marginalized and haphazard.

Lesson-based curriculums blend relationships;
they don't build them.

Community comes before learning. A framework of curriculum can't stand on a wet, cracked, or incomplete foundation of connections. Schools are spending millions of dollars on great curriculums that are supposed to teach initiatives, but these curriculums don't tell us how to build the relationships that make students want to learn and transfer that knowledge to their real lives. There is not a go-to, universal bag of tools for how to make the personal connections and relationships that keep students coming back to the classroom when things get tough.

Without stable school connections as a foundation for learning, no matter how great the initiative looks on paper, it fails in practice. If a student doesn't trust us, they can't learn from us. They won't see us as role models. They won't care. They'll resist. According to Trynia Kaufman, senior manager of editorial research at Understood, "Students' brains are hard at work every moment of the day, learning skills and connecting new information with old. Those same brains are also constantly processing information when it comes to their relationship with you, their teacher."[3]

But once critical connections are built throughout the classroom community, strengthening and aligning that community, challenges can be met and mitigated. Love conquers all, especially with students. They'd rather be with us than against us. All we need is a rock-solid foundation to stand on and a way to get there.

So how do we intentionally create a space where we're constantly putting connections before content? Connections before corrections? How do we intentionally and consistently find ways to put relationships before anything else?

Connection-Driven Classroom

The Connection-Driven Classroom (CDC) and its Teacher Connection Toolkit (TCT) is a research-based pedagogical framework aimed at managing student behavior by training educators in the art of forging, cultivating, and maintaining critical connections in the classroom through proactive and practical tools that take less than two minutes to use.

I'll go into more depth on the origin story of CDC later, but for

---

[3] https://www.understood.org/en/articles/brain-science-says-4-reasons-to-build-positive-relationships-with-students

now, know that it came out of several initiatives, including social-emotional learning (SEL) and restorative practices. A foundational element of the approach emphasizes strengthening relationships and community bonds. Then the proactive aspect of restorative practices builds a positive climate and relational base before conflicts arise. Combined, you have not only a resource that helps to effectively manage issues when they occur but also one that plays a significant role in preventing many conflicts from happening in the first place. There's also a touch of adverse childhood experiences (ACEs) and trauma-informed practices perched on the edges of the CDC conversation.

So the CDC is a hybrid of these initiatives, but what separates our philosophy, tools, product, and services from other initiatives is that we aren't curriculum based. You're never going to have to overhaul your day and condense your lesson plans to make room for our tools. You're never going to get a workbook or software that says, "Objective 1: Read this for ten minutes and have students do this activity." Our tools are non-lesson, Get to Know You (GTKY) based—four tools that take less than two minutes to do no matter what subject matter or grade level is being taught. We even use timers. They fit anywhere you want them, as needed. And all of our structures have one outcome: cross-connecting.

That is what sets our tools apart: the focus on cross-connections. And these cross-connections can't just happen once or twice and be expected to hold against hard cases and challenging content. The intentional effort and action to connect students with students, students with teachers, and teachers with students, must occur not just once or over the course of the first week of class but over and over again throughout the year. That effort and action creates a triangle of relationships that keeps getting stronger every time a connection is made or remade.

The Cross-Connection of Classroom Community Building =

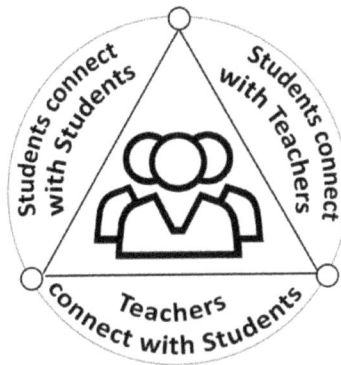

Most people, 70 to 80 percent of us, unintentionally leave out one side of the cross-connection triangle—student to student, student to teacher, teacher to student. If you're in the 10 to 15 percent who have "it," who automatically and intentionally include all three, this book is only going to confirm what you already know and do. For the majority of us, this book is a revelatory mindset shift that will allow us to teach more effectively and efficiently by using the CDC as a bedrock for all the other initiatives and content that need to be taught.

It's this layering of connections that increases students' engagement and cooperation in the classroom, increasing classroom productivity and success. It makes for a healthier classroom community that absorbs tension and heads off problems before they get too big. Students come to their educators when something comes up, trusting that they can help and won't reject them for their vulnerability. There's more trust. And where there's more trust, there is more learning and less discipline needed.

To trust each other, we need to know each other. To believe in each other, we need to know each other. To have difficult conversations about race and diversity and culture, every student in the classroom needs to first know they will be valued, seen, and heard for who they are and what they bring. And not just in beginning-of-the-year Getting to Know You activities but in all content conversations.

Our user-friendly experiential TCT tools create, cultivate, and maintain connections through simple tools and best practices that ultimately help all students in the classroom—all the community members in the classroom—feel valued, seen, and heard through cross-connections. These tools show us we're more alike than different in the struggles we go through and that it's not about pulling yourself up by your own bootstraps or grit but pulling *each other* up by hands and hearts. When the whole classroom community is in it together, we'll get there together.

Kaufman helps us understand what is happening in children's brains that allows classrooms to become safe spaces of learning. "Social activities like talking and laughing cause the body to release the hormone oxytocin. This helps us to bond with others. Those bonds create a feeling that's often called 'psychological safety'" When students feel psychologically safe, they're more likely to participate in class discussions, ask questions, try to do an assignment even when it's hard, or talk in a tone of voice that's appropriate for the situation."[4]

I'll say it again: we are not providing a curriculum for schools to adopt. Rather, it's an adaptable toolbox. A model of best practices that can be layered into any everyday classroom. The action here has been simplified to four tools that take two minutes or less to do but save a whole lot of time, energy, and heartbreak.

How Do I Know the Tools Work?

My company, Differentiated Discipline, formerly National Educators for Restorative Practices (NEDRP), provides two main pathways for school professional development. The first, and the one this book is about, is the CDC and its TCT, which teaches educators how to proactively create and cultivate connections in their classrooms. The second pathway is disrupting discipline,

---

[4] Trynia Kaufman, MS. "Building Positive Relationships with Students: What Brain Science Says." Understood. Accessed July 25, 2024. https://www.understood.org/en/articles/brain-science-says-4-reasons-to-build-positive-relationships-with-students.

which provides school leaders with strategies that focus on student accountability. Since these two things are related and often cross over, you'll be getting some of the big ideas that root both pathways, but just know that's not what you'll be tested on.

My team helps me run workshops and execute and improve, but the founding philosophy and mission came from my experiences and convictions. The tools I'm about to give you came from years of development, both leading up to my exit from the campus and afterward, when, cog-free, I took the leap, swam upstream, and started consulting on restorative practices.

At the time of this writing, I have a small team of educators and a home office in Austin, Texas. We're now a national educational company, supporting schools in building a foundation that focuses on the concrete of connections. Over the last nine years, we've trained over 30,000 educators. We founded the CDC mindset, and we're one of the few companies that teach educators how to connect with students and provide the exact tools to do so. Yes, the pieces look familiar, but they've been assembled into a model that's greater than the sum of its parts because it has an outcome: cross-connect.

This book grew out of the workshops my team and I do with schools around the country to cultivate learning environments where teachers can teach and students can learn by teaching these tools. Since we're private and not attached directly to a state or federal education system and bureaucracy, we're nimbler and more fluid. We can listen to educators and school leaders and adapt our training to what they need at their time and in their place. In other words, when it comes to discipline and behavior, we can meet you where you are at.

I like math (which I taught in addition to all the science classes), so I like to add things. I like to permutate and recombine. I like to evolve with my environment. So this is a dynamic model of practice that adapts with you and the time and energy you have to give it. The tools have been tailored to cut out as much of the work and energy required to use them as possible.

The big thing I want to provide you, as educators on the ground, in this book is the tools that will help you with students. That's the front line for academic and behavioral problems, and the best way to handle discipline is to take away the need for it.

Put another way by a principal who attended our training with a group of his teachers, "I've told my educators for twenty years the importance of building relationships with students, and what they're leaving with here today is the how."

That's what we're giving you: not your *why* but your *how*.

If what you're hearing speaks your language, this book—no, this *community*—is for you.

But first, to trust me and the big ideas and small tools I'm about to lay out, you may want to get to know me a little better. *#ConnectB4Content.*

Part I
The Story of CDC and its TCT

Chapter 1
A Little (More) about Me

No significant learning occurs without a significant relationship.

—James Comer

I'm the baby of a family of five. My next oldest sibling is eight and a half years my senior. My siblings love to call me "the Accident." I prefer the moniker "the Surprise." My mom just saved the best for last.

My mom was a food stamp caseworker. She was a rock. When my nieces and nephews struggled with addiction, my mom, their grandma, always let them stay at her house when they got kicked out of their own. I had a hard time with her sympathy. I'll help my family with rehab, but I can't bring myself to bail them out. I feel as if I'd be supporting their mistakes. I had encouraged my mom to do the same. "One day," she told me, "you'll understand." More on this later but excuse me a moment while I shed a tear or two.

My dad was another story. When he retired from the military after twenty-seven years, he decided to work on the road. I was left to be parented by my mom with some visits with my dad. I was seven. When he came back to officially join us, I was fifteen, and he tried to pick up where he'd left off, telling me what to do. We clashed. Of course we did. He'd broken my trust when I was young and didn't know how to get it back. He loved the fact that I was an athlete and got good grades. He loved to say, "I've got a great student on the field." He loved to say, "My son plays football and baseball." And he loved to come to my games. But there was something fundamental about my personality and dreams—about our relationship—he just didn't get.

I loved my father, but I didn't respect him. I was left with this feeling that I wasn't good enough for him to stay. In my childhood brain, I concluded he just didn't want *me*.

And that's what really underlies the mantra of valued, seen, and heard. These actions fulfill a need for people, especially students. The need to be wanted. To connect. To belong.

My older brothers stepped into the gap while my dad was gone and became my primary male influences. Every summer, I lived with one of my siblings in some form or fashion because my mom couldn't afford a babysitter while I was out of school. What made this a little difficult was that my brothers were recreational drug and alcohol users. At nine, I was introduced to marijuana. At twelve, I snorted my first line of cocaine. My parents hadn't promoted this lifestyle, but it was my reality, as complex as any of the realities for our students.

What made a difference for me was my teachers. In fourth grade, Ms. Bagby and others knew I wanted to be the smartest, the fastest, the best. I wanted to stand out in a positive way. I was the shiny, bright student who wanted to please. Wanted to belong. My teachers fed that yearning. If I got done with my work early, they let me go help the younger students. To me, it was a sweet deal. I remember asking Ms. Bagby, "Is this what it feels like to be a teacher?" And when she responded yes, I was hooked. I wanted to be a teacher and help people learn.

The positive path my teachers set me on made me an outlier in my family. My brothers wouldn't even cut their hair to play football, and here I was throwing myself into school sports and academics. Those things filled my bucket more than any quick fix my brothers offered. And as I grew older, I started noticing how the drugs negatively affected their lives: petty theft, jail, rehab. I decided I didn't want to be like that.

I graduated with the highest GPA of all male athletes at my high school of three thousand students. It allowed me to walk on to a college football team on an academic scholarship. Then I found out quickly I wasn't going to be the next star athlete and win a Heisman. I came back home after a year and went on the pay-as-you-go, part-time school route. I stuck with college because I wanted to be an educator.

My brothers' paths continued to diverge. Eventually, all three of my oldest brothers lost their lives, in reverse order of their births. The next oldest to me died when his heart stopped while he was smoking marijuana as he did every day. The middle brother died from HIV and hepatitis C, contracted when he shared needles. The oldest, who cut me my first line of cocaine, died from carbon monoxide poisoning after coming home from partying and passing out in his still-running car after the garage door closed. The authorities say it wasn't suicide, but the rough life he led definitely factored in.

So why am I telling you all this? Because it explains why I am here today, doing the work I am doing. It shows how we don't really know a person until we know them—until we value, see, and hear the lived experiences that make them who they are and drive what they do. That even a student with enough adverse childhood experiences to put him at risk can still be resilient if he gets support somewhere.

My parents did the best they could with the tools and resources they had available to them. But it was my teachers and coaches who made the biggest impact, who shaped me into the healthy and functional person I am today. My parents praised me for what I did, but my teachers and coaches encouraged me to do more. To be more.

Yes, I grew up with deficits. But I also grew up with educators who valued, saw, and heard my assets: my drive, my intelligence, and my need to contribute. My teachers and coaches provided role models, father figures, and accountability. They related and connected. I used that foundation to build a house that wouldn't fall.

That's what led me to education. It's why I'm speaking to you now.

At First, I Taught

I have twenty-six years in education: elementary school, middle school, and high school. I've occupied roles including principal, assistant principal, classroom teacher, instructional coach, and high school football coach. As an offensive coordinator for football and head coach for baseball, I learned a balance between discipline and relationships. I learned how to shape and grow a child into a full person while also caring about and relating to that person.

When you look at my DNA, the D stands for discipline.

When you look at my RNA, the R stands for relationships.

With that joke, you shouldn't be surprised that when I taught, I taught integrated physics, biology, chemistry, speech, health, physical education, and one year of sixth-grade math. In other words, in this book, I still wear my corny science educator humor on my...sleeves. I spent ten years in the classroom before going over to the other side.

Yes, I became an administrator. But I didn't leave teaching; I just switched to teaching adults, which is harder than teaching students. And before you shake your head at me, think about all the biases, preconceived notions, and fixed mindsets that we carry around with us as we age. Our brains become less plastic. It's harder for us to be open to new ways of doing things and change ingrown practices. As a learner coming to this book hoping for a better way, you've already taken the first step.

So where did this education and experience in relational and restorative practices come from? Well, I happened to be on the first campus in the state of Texas to implement a school-wide restorative discipline (RD) approach at Ed White Middle School in San Antonio, Texas. The program allowed me to loop up with my students from sixth through eighth grades, which meant I could be a consistent father figure for my students. As the students were going through the program, we partnered with the Institute of Restorative Justice and Restorative Dialogue at the University of Texas at Austin. They did a three-year study and evaluation on the program as the first cohort of students matriculated through to high school.[5]

---

[5] You can learn all about the findings of that study here: https://irjrd.org/wp-content/uploads/2016/01/Year-3-FINAL-Ed-White-report.pdf

The Texas Education Agency (TEA) then partnered with UT at Austin to do training throughout the state based on the successful program. They recruited me to share my experiences with students and be the spokesperson for the program, which required me to leave my school and teaching career. I was in a consultant role and guaranteed no salary, no benefits—nothing but faith and the idea that restorative practices were a critical need for both educators and students.

Across the state, the TEA had twenty education service centers, professional development hubs at which to hold training that were already in place across the state. They targeted regions that had the most disproportionate rates of exclusion of minority students as the starting point for the training, and I was in charge of leading those trainings. Two years passed before we completed the Texas tour. In the meantime, I could also work with schools individually, doing training and consultations and setting up my own business for and with the service centers.

During that time, Dr. Gaye Lang from TEA invited me to collaborate on a book based on the implementation of the program in Texas. That was when I became a coauthor of *Restorative Discipline Practices: A Journey of Implementation by a Community of Texas Educators*. I contributed a chapter from the administrator's perspective, sharing what it was like to implement it for the first time.

The Infamous Ed White Middle School

The first time I implemented restorative practices was at Ed White Middle School in San Antonio. For those familiar with Texas schools, yes, *the* Ed White. When I started there, the school was infamous for high discipline, low morale, and a distrustful campus community. Not the school you'd want to put in for, but I wasn't thinking about that when I was hired. I had been an assistant principal for two years at Schertz Elementary in Schertz-Cibolo-Universal City (SCUC) ISD. Then I went to Karnes City ISD at Karnes City Junior High for two years as a principal. It was a rural school of two hundred sixty students, and I commuted one hundred fifty miles round trip every day. Ed White was twenty-five minutes from my house; I wanted to return to San Antonio. Its school district, the Northeast Independent School District (NE ISD), had sixty-seven thousand students enrolled in 2011. I would be going back to being an assistant principal but in a much larger district.

We have a connection problem that
is disguised as a discipline problem.

Ed White had one thousand students, sixth through eighth grades—50 percent Hispanic, 30 percent African American, 10 percent white—and it also had a 65 percent mobility rate (which counts when a student withdraws and a student comes in). Translation: high turnover of the student population throughout the school year; we lost a lot of students to gain ten. Ninety-three percent of students' families qualified socioeconomically as low-income. There was a 60 percent turnover in core teaching areas before the pandemic.

All these challenges made for low trust and few connections. Students displayed resistance and pushed back on educators to see if they would leave. If the educator came back the next year, the students were all smiles. Abandonment and loss are high among low-income student populations, so when educators come back in the face of resistance, they solidify stability, and the students trust them. No one wants to form a relationship with someone who will leave at the first sign of trouble, and sometimes pushback is the only control the students have—they reject you before you reject them.

Again, value, see, and hear me, even when I tell you I don't want you to.

Resistance all day is hard for anyone to take. For all my cajoling and reassurance that the students would come around, I'd have educators walk out in the middle of the day, totally overwhelmed, and not come back.

This was before the pandemic. Turnover among all educator populations now is higher across the board, from substitutes and older educators no longer willing to take risks with their health to educators getting farmed out to other schools to emotional burnout. All contribute to a mass exodus from the profession and an increasing educator shortage.

Unfortunately, the result is even more intractable and distrustful student populations. A mass lack of cross-connections and relationships—which directly impacts student engagement and cooperation in the classroom—makes for a toxic community.

Of course, our biggest evaluation factor in every school system is content accountability. Ed White in 2011 didn't meet district accountability, state accountability, or federal accountability. Our scores were so low we couldn't even spell *accountability* on our tests. The word was too big for us. And that wasn't just a joke. We identified that 56 percent of our students were at least two grade levels behind in reading. If students can't read to grade level and their math scores are low, they're going to struggle on any state assessment.

So we had one thousand students showing up every day, half of whom struggled academically. What do students do when they have a weakness and can't understand the lesson? And when they don't trust their educators or peers enough to ask for help? They act out.

Resistance was everywhere. And early in my regime, resistance was futile.

I'm a former cyborg of suspensions. I'm embarrassed about how I used to talk to students. I used to tell students to "kick rocks," as in kick rocks while they walked home. I used to tell students, "You're suspended," and when their moms would admit to not having enough gas money to pick them up and no other relatives were available, I'd stand firm. I'd tell them, "That's okay. But I have to get your son off campus. All I need is permission for him to walk home." Manipulated and without a choice, Mom would consent.

I'd take the student, usually a boy, to the front office. I'd sign him out. I'd walk him to the front of the school, and he'd ask, "So what am I supposed to do?"

"What does your mom's text message say?"

"Walk home. But I live three miles from here."

"Not my problem. In fact, let me make it easier for you. I'm going to walk you off this curb. The school property ends at this curb. Once I walk you off, if you come back on, that's a criminal trespass warning. If you continue to walk on, that's a route to juvenile detention. Make your move."

That's how I was taught to do student discipline. My job was to kick students out of school. And I was good at it.

We ended up leading the district with 1,149 suspensions, including in-school, out-of-school, and partial-day. Our answer to a student's rejection of us was to reject them in turn. We were the number-one exclusionary campus in our district. This was definitely not the number-one we wanted to celebrate. But it stemmed from a philosophy of discipline that's as old as the public school system itself: pull your weeds.

I'd been charged by my principal with running the "back end" of the school, a common charge for assistant principals, which basically meant I was the one in charge of meting out consequences for bad behavior. And the school's philosophy for running the back end was to get rid of the students who "didn't want to be there" so the students who did could learn. It viewed the campus like a garden. If you have weeds that don't do any good and deprive resources from your productive plants, you pull them. The thinking is that what's left is the flowers that can bloom.

But if you treat a student like a weed and talk to a student like a weed, then they'll act like a weed. On top of that, weeding out the "bad students" actually doesn't allow the other flowers to bloom.

In his profound work, "Note to Educators: Hope Required When Growing Roses in Concrete," Jeff Duncan-Andrade provides a poignant analogy that challenges the traditional disciplinary approaches often adopted in educational settings. He writes, "We may think that if we send out the 'disobedient' child, we have removed the pain from our system...we rationalize the exclusion by telling ourselves that we have pulled a weed from the garden, allowing for a healthier environment for the other children to grow." This metaphor beautifully captures the flawed rationale behind exclusionary practices in education.

Duncan-Andrade's analogy invites us to reconsider how we perceive and handle challenging behaviors in the classroom. Removing a student as though they are a weed suggests a permanent solution to a temporary problem, falsely simplifying the school's complex ecosystem.

Jeff Duncan-Andrade further enriches the dialogue on educational inclusion by referencing his colleague, K. Wayne Yang, who profoundly states, "All my students are indigenous to my classroom, and therefore, there are no weeds in my classroom." This powerful affirmation is a cornerstone for rethinking how we view and treat all students within the educational landscape.

By understanding and internalizing the principle that there are no weeds in our classrooms, we challenge ourselves to rethink and reshape our teaching practices. Jeff Duncan-Andrade's and K. Wayne Yang's perspectives invite us to build educational environments grounded in respect, inclusion, and equity. In a Connection-Driven Classroom, this belief becomes a guiding principle, ensuring every student is seen as a valuable and indispensable part of the community. Let this belief in the absence of weeds inspire us to cultivate a garden where every type of flower can bloom beautifully, reflecting the diversity and potential of our students.[6]

Our weed pulling of 1,149 suspensions led to a pause. Central office representatives came in and had a conversation with us. The data showed we led the district with suspensions, but the real kicker was that the negative behaviors the suspensions were supposed to stop were not stopping. In fact, our negative behaviors were increasing. It was the first time we looked at the data and saw starkly that the good we thought we were doing by toeing the line didn't exist. In fact, we were doing active harm. We were living out repeating the same mistakes and expecting different results.

I seriously considered quitting then and there. At that point in education, I lost my why—why I was in education. That fourth-

[6] Singapore-MIT Alliance. "Course Materials." Su09. Accessed July 25, 2024. http://web.mit.edu/sma/courses/materials/Su09.htm.

grade boy who only wanted to help students be better, to make a positive difference, was now going toe to toe with students, yelling at students, kicking students out of school. And nothing good came out of it for the other students. I was not the person I wanted to be.

The school system can shape you into what it needs you to be. And at that time and place, it needed me to be an exclusionary consequence guy. I typed up a letter of resignation and talked to my principal. He said, "I'm not going to take this right now. You need to think about it."

Students believe teachers leave the parking lot each day thinking they made a big difference in education and have a lot of money.

How often have you sat in your vehicle in the parking lot before going home, just to take a moment? You start to reflect. *Did I make a difference today?* Exhausted, you scramble through your mind to grasp at least one impactful thing from the day. You eventually drive home, and you don't even remember the drive. You're on autopilot. Numb. And then you get home, and you're thinking about your students. Worrying about your students. Worrying about your job and job performance. Worrying that you've somehow failed as an educator. That you're an imposter, doing more harm than good.

It's an indescribable despair.

These have always been burdens educators carry—ten times more so in the aftermath of COVID-19.

You get home, and the other person in your house—in my case, my wife, an elementary school principal at a non-title I campus with very few discipline problems and plenty of parental support—has no idea. They jump in cheerfully, "Let me tell you about the day I've had!"

And you're thinking, *Please no.*

"A few fourth-grade students came to my office and surprised me with a cup of coffee and read me a story. During announcements, since we are a bilingual school, we did the Pledge of Allegiance in Spanish, and then I had all the classrooms do the Cupid shuffle!"

Now let me tell you about my day. Two mamas in pajamas in the parking lot cursed me out before I walked into the office. I had no idea who they were or what part I played in their situation. When I made it into the building, their students were already waiting at my office to get disciplined for this or that. I had this many in-school suspensions. I had this many manifestation determinations. I had this many hearing packets. I didn't get to walk through any educational classrooms because I was putting out fires and talking to angry parents all day long, and I didn't even realize till now that I didn't even eat lunch. That's my day.

And that was why I wanted to quit.

But my principal wanted to try something different. His wife was a criminal justice major taking a class at the University of Texas at San Antonio from an adjunct professor named Robert Rico. He had twenty-nine years of criminal justice experience in a town just west of San Antonio. He found he was arresting the same youths over and over and over again and thought, *There's got to be something different.* He researched restorative justice, which outlines an approach to criminal discipline where the perpetrator is *restored* or included back in the community.

For example, say you break into a car. Instead of being just thrown in jail, you're given the opportunity to sit down and look the person you've wronged in the eye, have a conversation with them, and hear how your choice impacted them and others. That conversation is led by an impartial facilitator. Then you have to come to an agreement about what you're going to do to make amends.

This model had been applied to schools in Oakland, California, in a program called Restorative Justice for Oakland Youth (RJOY). Rico thought the same concepts could be applied to our school. We could be the first restorative campus in the state of Texas.

So the administrative team had a conversation about what we could do in our school. I was listening to this conversation with my unaccepted letter of resignation on my principal's desk. He turned to me and said, "Kevin, you would be great at this."

"I don't understand. Great at what?"

"This is about keeping students in school versus kicking them out. It's about building relationships. It's about getting to know your students. It's about all these things."

"That doesn't describe our current school system."

He paused. "Yes, it would have to be something completely different."

Still feeling the fringes of despair, I said, "I don't even know what that would look like."

But I was willing to try it anyway.

I'd be the first restorative discipline coordinator in Texas. A pilot project with fifteen teachers, starting with sixth grade and three hundred students. One-third of the campus would be introduced to a whole different mindset. And I was tasked with leading it.

To codify this experiment, we partnered with the Institute of Restorative Justice and Restorative Dialogue at the University of Texas at Austin. This allowed us to lean into the experiences of Dr. Marilyn Armor, Stephanie Frogge, and Robert Rico, who came to teach us about restorative justice, the theory our pilot program would center around. But we'd have to answer my concern: what would this social theory look like in a school? At first, we called it restorative discipline.

But before we go into the theories and the inspiration that would lead to the CDC, I first want to make my motives for telling you all this clear.

It's about Conviction

I was going to be a youth pastor. It felt like God was moving me in that direction. I know not all of us may practice a religion or have positive growth experiences through faith, but it was important to my development.

I was struggling to keep up with my master's program, and after a year and a half, I pulled out of it. But I realized, as I got into restorative work, that the ministry I thought God had prepared me for was really this teaching. I used to come into the room with a concept of restorative discipline gleaned through my personal experience, and it was my way or the highway. *What do you mean you don't believe it will work? Didn't you see my video? Didn't you see my data?* I'd get defensive and, yes, exclusionary. Again, something that's supposed to be anathema to restorative practices.

But then God softened my heart. Through discipleship, God taught me transformation begins not from my efforts to convert others but through their own inner conviction. Discipleship illuminated for me that true change blossoms from within, from a heart that's open and willing. It taught me the power of an invitation over compulsion, highlighting the receptivity that comes with being invited rather than forced.

In the realm of faith, conviction stands as a deep-seated belief, a certainty in the truth that resonates within one's core. This concept of conviction extends beyond mere acceptance—it embodies an unwavering belief in what is true.

Professionally, my compensation isn't tied to the number of people I persuade. Regardless of whether my audience embraces change, my remuneration remains constant. Similarly, the value of this book is inherent, unaffected by its condition—be it well used or neglected.

My role isn't to convert, convince, or condemn you for your current practices. Nor is it to instigate change within you; after all, changing others, be they students or adults, is beyond my capabilities. My purpose is to inspire a shift in perspective on how we approach student behavior management. Echoing Socrates' wisdom, "I cannot teach anybody anything. I can only make them think," I aim to provoke thought.

To foster this reflective journey, I will navigate through three pivotal domains: the mind (head), the emotions (heart), and the actions (hands). My discussions will intertwine factual information, personal experiences, and practical tools, aiming to enrich your understanding, touch your heart, and empower your actions.

And these points will weigh the scales toward a personal decision to consider change—or not.

Think about your mindset right at this moment.

We come to this work, this book, with our biases and beliefs already in place. Raise your hand if you want change.

Now raise your hand if you want *to* change. That one may be harder to answer.

John Maxwell says, "Change is inevitable, but growth is intentional." That's how human minds work.

Here's an example to clarify. Cross your arms. Yes, I know, you have to put the book or tablet down. If you have a hard copy of this book, you have to weigh the pages somehow so it doesn't flip closed. I'll wait...all set now? Okay, arms crossed. Is that comfortable? Yeah? All right. Do me a favor: flip your arms over and cross them the other way. I'll give you another moment. Now how does that feel? Maybe a little uncomfortable? Maybe a little unnatural? Exactly.

Let's go back to that quote: "Change is inevitable, but growth is intentional." When I asked you to cross your arms, you didn't have to think about it the first time. It's baked into your DNA and how you've learned to move your body since being a student.

As for me, I used to be a nose-to-nose, toes-to-toes type of person. I used to love getting into people's bubbles. I got triggered by the three D's: defiance, disrespect, and disobedience. I'd react. I was a high school varsity football coach. That face mask was as close as I could get to you without being in your face. That is my historical DNA.

So how did I go from someone who would tell students to kick rocks to, three years later, telling students, "I love you. You're suspended today. Let me take you home. Let's make sure you get a haircut. Let's make sure that when you come back tomorrow, I'm the first person to meet you after your suspension because I want you to know that you belong here and that today's suspension doesn't define you. It's a blip. A hiccup. A small grain of sand on the beach of your life."

The answer is simple: thoughtful practice.

Growth is intentional. You had to intentionally use your mind to cross your arms the other way because you're not used to doing it that way. It's uncomfortable because your body isn't used to that movement and that position, but it doesn't mean it's the wrong way. Just different.

I'm just trying to get you to cross your arms in a different way—to think differently. But notice that the outcome is still crossing your arms. With practice, before you know it, you're crossing your arms the other way, and it's not as bad. You've trained your brain to do it. It's just repetition, like learning a second language or a sport. You feel awkward going through those poses or strategies because you've never done it before. Until your amygdala gives you positive reinforcement for doing things differently, you're not going to be able to easily cross your arms in a different way.

That's the mindset. I can't change you permanently. That's your decision and your journey. I just want you to understand the purpose behind what I'm sharing with you throughout this book. And if you can tolerate being uncomfortable for a moment, I want you to practice in a different way.

It's an Inside Job

My faith taught me people come to God through a relationship. They come on their own terms, and they come in their own way. They are not pushed or forced. That's what I thought I had to do to get people to change. But they have to feel intrinsically motivated—motivated from the inside—to change.

Changes in mindset are also like that.

If this book doesn't lead to a new conviction for you, I'm not mad. I don't take it personally. I hope you are doing something great. I hope that you are being successful with your students. I hope that you are satisfied. And if this book makes you pause and wonder, "Could I do something different?" That's even better.

Again, I'm not here to convert, convince, or condemn. But I will say this.

I have hundreds of stories of educators admitting to me that they were going to retire. That they were burned out and overwhelmed. That they were on antidepressants because of their jobs. And the tools they learned in one of our training sessions gave them light in the darkness, a new energy for their work, and a positive outlook. These tools have literally gotten educators off drugs.

If nothing else, they could take a pause and a breath and realize they weren't failing the system; the system was failing them. They realized they could connect with their students, build relationships—and do it in a way that fit within their curriculum and within a normal school day.

I'm not here to make money. Trust me, the motive for writing and publishing your own book is *not* to get rich. I'm not even here to share my expertise. It's not like I went to school for this work. But I am experienced. I have years' worth of trial and error to bring to you.

Often, a book or story is shared in an effort to make a difference. That is the goal of this book. If you find one tool in this book that makes a difference to one student in your classroom, then this book is worth all the time, effort, and vulnerability put into it, both for me as the author and you as the reader.

That's what fills my bucket now. Helping educators help students. And maybe that was my real motivation as that fourth-grade boy. It wasn't just helping students; it was helping my *educators* help students—just as I now want to help you be the best version of yourself. I want you to be able to take joy in your job, to have your bucket filled, too, so you have the energy and ability to help as many students—students like me—as possible.

Chapter 2
Relationships vs. Connections

When they think about building relationships in the classroom, most educators think, I naturally do this as part of my teaching. Others may think, I don't have time for this. Recently, a staff member shared something that I had never considered before. She said, "I am fine connecting with over a hundred students, but I don't have the time or energy to build relationships with over a hundred students."

Wow! I had never stopped long enough to consider the differences between those two words: connections vs. relationships. Some educators even go as far as saying that the phrase "relationship-building" can be triggering.

Meanwhile, I have used those terms interchangeably, almost as synonyms for each other. However, after considering the possible differences, something resonated with me at my core. I started to reflect on this perspective in my own life. As I'm writing this book, my wife and I have been married for a year and a half. We met on Facebook, created a connection, and started dating. That connection rapidly increased, and we found ourselves engaged in just eighteen days and married on day fifty-eight. I know, crazy! But I began to see that it all started with a *connection* first. Then, it took the last year and a half to build a relationship. This relationship did take more time and energy.

Empathizing with educators, I now see and feel how the weight of the phrase "relationship-building" in a modern classroom, with so many other factors impacting their instruction, can be overwhelming. So let's think differently and scaffold that plan. Let's focus on creating a concrete base of connections in the classroom and let any potential relationship-building naturally stack on this firm foundation. Opening our minds to this subtle shift in how we approach these terms can make a huge difference in our ability to be more open-minded to implementing these strategies.

Everybody has their go-to relationship-building activity, things like "Two Truths and a Lie," sharing a presentation on their family, or a poster of who they are. There are so many activities to choose from.

Honestly, I have never given too much thought about what activities teachers leaned into to create connections in the classroom. But asking a teacher, "What are your go-to relationship activities?" led me to experience one of my most significant two-by-four moments during an afternoon break while training in Pflugerville, Texas. It was 2:40 p.m., and I'd just popped a Dr. Pepper for a caffeinated push to make it to the end of the day. A teacher approached me, sharing, "I love today's training, and I do things like this in my classroom all the time." As I thanked him, we struck up a casual conversation. By chance, I asked, "What is your go-to relationship-building activity?" (Remember that I had not asked this question before I started this work.)

He paused and replied, "The old brown-bag autobiography. Are you familiar with it?"

I sipped my Dr. Pepper and said, "Of course. I love that activity!" If you don't know it, a brown-bag autobiography activity is a form of show-and-tell for students to get to know each other better. Students are assigned to bring five items from home and stick these objects in a brown paper bag. There are usually criteria for what kind of objects to include. In class, everyone takes a turn unpacking their bag and explaining why they chose them. "I assume that when your students share, the other students love learning about what's in the brown bags."

He replied, "They love learning about each other."

"I'll also assume," I continued, "that, as the teacher, you watch the students present their bags. And you learn about the students."

He confirmed, "That is my favorite part! I even have a sheet where I record all the items to refer to. I learn so much about my students during this activity."

So I asked him, "What do you put in your brown paper bag?"

He responded, "Nothing. I don't do a brown bag."

I didn't automatically condemn him, but as a self-described teacher who loves these activities, I naturally became curious. "So why didn't you share your brown bag?"

"Because the directions didn't tell me to," he replied so matter-of-factly that it was like a board striking me across the forehead. Wait. What?

At that moment, I realized that we must be specific with the directions in our relationship-building activities. We must prompt teachers when students should share with other students. We must prompt teachers when they should listen to students. And we must prompt teachers when teachers should share with students. I couldn't wait to share this revelation with my staff. This exchange changed how we intentionally unpacked our tools for staff members moving forward, all due to a casual conversation over a break in training.

Conversely, if you are a teacher and you just paused in your gut and asked, "Why *wouldn't* I do a brown bag as a teacher?" I want to assure you that you aren't the norm; you're the exception. The people who naturally include themselves in relationship-building activities are about 10 to 15 percent of the population. There's another 10 percent of educators who will never even consider including themselves, no matter what, and who are probably in education for the wrong reasons. But the rest, that 70 to 80 percent, just never received the best guidance for the activity.

Think about it from this perspective. Teachers are great soldiers. Just tell us what to do. Tell us what's best for the mission. Tell us what we're going to be evaluated on. Tell us how much we're going to get paid. Just tell us, and we'll follow through on it. We're really good soldiers. But what's interesting is that when you look up instructions for doing brown-bag activities, they never specifically tell the educator to share a brown bag of their own. This cross-connection is left out of the instructions.

So one reason teachers don't share is *we were never told*. Educators aren't to blame for their mindsets. We're just following instructions. Doing what the Powers That Be think is best practice. And, as educators, we're *good* at following instructions. So any little judgment others lodge against educators, or that educators lodge against themselves, of falling short on the inclusion and connection gets corrected right here and now.

For any relationship-building activity, we must ask ourselves: what's the intention here? Was this activity chosen at random? How often is the activity done? How much time does it take? What is the outcome afterward, and is it the outcome we wanted?

Triangle of Cross-Connections

Student to student, student to teacher, teacher to student—that triangle of connections is key. If all the sides are connected, students treat each other better. They treat the teacher better. The teacher treats the students better. The consistent outcomes for all the TCT tools I'm about to introduce is that triangle and the better behavior, participation, and learning that come from its sides being reinforced again and again and again. This is the return on your investment in connections. Our data supports that most teachers who implement with fidelity experience an average 50 percent reduction in classroom disruption.

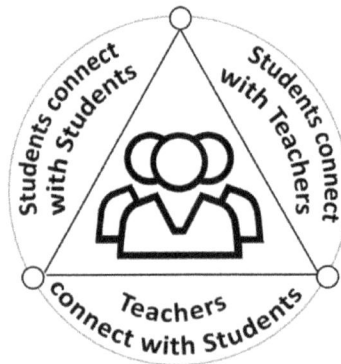

If we continue with this metaphor, a triangle is also one of the strongest shapes there is. In architecture, it's used all the time. So what better structure to hold us up?

If we use that triangle to weave relationships for all our students and each connection is a thread or piece of yarn or rope, soon we've built a strong safety net. If something goes sideways, if things get tough, for one strand or many, the whole structure ensures the rest won't fall. Think of a spider's web. A fly can bust through it, tear up individual strands, bring all sorts of havoc, but the web doesn't lose its moorings. The total structure doesn't fall. Each strand is built to pull on the others as needed, and that makes it stronger. That's what we're showing you how to construct. A web of cross-connections that make each individual strand stronger because of the neighboring strands it's tied to. If there were no other strands, if there was no one at the other end of the rope, and something big pulled on us, we'd fall.

That's what's happening in classrooms right now. We're not connected, at least not strongly. We don't know each other. Prior to the pandemic, I would have reflected on these gaps and said that we had cracks in our connections. Post-pandemic, I would have observed that those cracks have widened to canyons. Everything else is pressing and stressing us, and we never seem to have the time, energy, or capacity to do that relational work.

You can't strengthen something that doesn't exist. We can grab at curriculums and initiatives touted as the answers to all our problems, but if there's nothing to anchor those heavy lifts, if there's nothing to grab at the other end, we're just free falling.

Webs of connection are what help us stay together and not fall apart.

It's time for us to get out from behind our desks, those big barriers of authority, and sit among the students. We don't have to share our deepest secrets, but if we want to form connections, we must show our students we trust them with parts of our personal histories too.

Understanding the triangle of cross-connections in education is akin to mastering the art of laying the foundation for a solid classroom environment. The key takeaway from this model is the importance of comprehending that every effort invested in fostering connections within the school community should encompass three essential dimensions: student-to-student, student-to-educator, and educator-to-student interactions.

Capturing the Connection

At the end of each TCT, you will receive a prompt to Capture the Connection, akin to tying a bow on an academic lesson. The teacher concludes the tool by capturing genuine connections, spotlighting key insights gained about your students, what they discovered about you, and their learnings about each other.

Here, the true value of connections becomes apparent. Many teachers, having gone through the CDC training, realize they had previously overlooked the importance of student-to-student connections. By fostering and leveraging these relationships, staff members come to appreciate the significance of nurturing such cross-connections. As students learn more about each other, their treatment toward one another improves. Similarly, as students gain insights into their teacher, and as the teacher learns more about the students, mutual respect and treatment enhance. It's essential to capture a snapshot of these connections by using Capture the Connection at the end of each tool, making it a priority.

SEL and Other Initiatives

In education, we often prioritize initiatives aimed at addressing relational challenges. One of the latest approaches is social-emotional learning (SEL), spearheaded by CASEL (Collaborative for Academic, Social, and Emotional Learning). However, SEL faces criticism and scrutiny, with some advocating for its restriction or outright prohibition. Some even find a place for it in state political agendas. What is *not* controversial? Classrooms must establish connections with kids.

Yet my intention is not to condemn or endorse SEL. Instead, I aim to use it as a case-in-case to show how such initiatives might not deliver the desired results and outcomes we aspire to achieve.

SEL has five competencies:

1. Self-awareness
2. Self-management
3. Responsible decision-making
4. Social awareness
5. Relationship skills

If you think about it, though, relationship skills are embedded within the five other competencies. It's not the first on the SEL list. Maybe it should be.

The need for SEL initiatives existed before the pandemic. Going back into schools after the pandemic, when everything has just gone more haywire, made that need even more evident. Of course it did. Put even more stress and hardship, plus interrupted relationships, on top of an already shaky system, and it was bound to widen the cracks that were already there. Students now have increased needs for physical, mental, and emotional support. Their home lives are even more upended. They trust the learning experience even less. Some schools grasp SEL as the answer to their sinking ships. They buy and plunk down a huge chunk of abstract information delivered through software and expect it to work.

But how are we cross-connecting? How are we supporting the legs of that triangle? How are we strengthening all the connections in the classroom community? Do these curriculum-based activities create the connections that will help students be successful? Where are the assessments and accountability?

Students don't care what you know until they
know how much you care.
–John C. Maxwell

Now, I'm not here to bash lesson-based curriculums. They are important in their own right and head in the right direction. But we miss the boat when there is any curriculum without the connection. It is the connection that gets students to board the boat with us. If we don't know each other, we leak. The boat sinks. Or, in the worst-case scenario, no one gets on board at all.

These activities come at a cost and may not actually meet students' social-emotional needs in many cases. Your math, reading, and science scores are not actually improving along with these activities. How do we talk about emotional needs if we can't trust each other to handle that raw vulnerability? How do we talk about diversity and culture if we don't look or live like our students? If we don't know and trust each other, how are we going to address those sensitive subjects?

Here's what sets our tools apart from curriculum-based lessons:

- ✓ They're intentional.
- ✓ They're sustainable.
- ✓ They're systematic.
- ✓ They're manageable.
- ✓ They cross-connect.

TCT tools don't just patch rocky foundations. They build something altogether different. They pour concrete foundations. They provide the stability curriculums can be built on. Once you have the foundation, any curriculum you want to add to it—SEL, trauma informed, diversity, equity, inclusion, math, science, English—will have a solid base to stand on. If something goes sideways in an activity, if a window gets broken, it won't break the foundation. Rebuilding the classroom community becomes easier.

Simply put, put connections before initiatives. *#ConnectB4Content*

I'm not trying to compete with these initiatives, but there's nobody in front of SEL. There's nobody in front of diversity or culture initiatives. There's nobody telling you what to do or how to do it efficiently and effectively. And embedded in these initiatives are complex, complicated ideas rooted in emotions, culture, and identity. Touchy stuff for most of us to poke at. It's like a prickly pear cactus. It looks smooth, but go ahead and touch it, and your fingers are inflamed by tiny needles you can't even see to tweeze out.

Aside from SEL, there are a few other concepts schools rely on that share commonalities with the CDC. One of them is concerned with the research done around adverse childhood experiences (ACEs). ACEs have their own researchers and books and workshops, so I'm not going to go into them in this book. But in brief, ACEs catalog a set of childhood experiences, such as divorce, abuse, or addiction, that a person witnesses or goes through during their young life. A higher ACE score can lead to negative social and health outcomes in adulthood. But a higher score can be mitigated by several factors that lead to resilience in the face of these traumas, one of which (no surprise) is connection to even just one supportive person.

One day I hope to fully incorporate this theory, which has prompted alternative disciplinary approaches on other school campuses, especially in Washington state (see the documentary *Paper Tigers*). ACEs, as used in schools, emphasize acknowledging the root cause of a student's bad behavior, their traumas or adverse experiences, to form connections and reconnect plans. The CDC concentrates more on the flip side of that coin, on how to connect proactively with students even when you don't know their traumas. And, frankly, sometimes it's better for all of us not to get stuck in a student's unfortunate story so we don't create a negative bias around what we expect of that student.

Chapter 3
What Makes a Teacher Outstanding?

The influence of a good teacher can never be erased.
—Unknown

I don't feel like my students can be vulnerable."

A third-grade teacher dropped this confession on me as I was getting ready to model our next TCT activity for the class. She'd been practicing the TCT tools, and I was acting in my role as her support and coach. First, I would've liked to ask her why vulnerability was so important to her, since connections don't have to be deep, but let's just say vulnerability equaled authenticity here. So what she really meant was that her students were holding back.

Okay, so let's observe. When I first entered the classroom, I noticed the teacher sitting in a chair away from the space her students and I were using on the floor. This isn't unusual, especially when teachers feel they need to be in observation mode with a consultant, but for an activity centered on relationships, that physical distance becomes a big, yawning chasm.

As the activity got going, answering GTKY questions in a circle, the teacher remained apart. I even forced the issue with some experiential learning. I asked a student to hand the talking piece we were using to her teacher. After the teacher shared, she inched her chair closer to her students' space but kept some separation.

Not close enough.

Several rounds later, she was still in teaching mode, holding herself apart, and most of her conversation focused on redirecting behavior: "Put that down. This is the activity we're doing now. Hands to ourselves." She was not in listening mode.

I needed to get her attention. The next round, I pulled out the big kahuna. "You have one wish, but you can only wish that wish for someone else. When it's your turn, say the name of the person you are wishing for and what that wish is." I modeled an answer, and we went around again.

"Mom, I wish you had a big house."

"Grandpa, I wish you could go fishing."

"Carly, I wish you were still here."

This last wish was from a young boy who didn't say anything more as the talking piece got passed again, but when we finished with the activity, and I was high-fiving and thanking all the students, I crossed paths with that young boy, and I offered a follow-up: "So tell me more about Carly."

"She was my cousin and died in a house fire."

Deep breath time. "Thank you," I said and gave him a hug. We took a selfie.

As the teacher walked me to the door, I said, "Today, when I came in here, you mentioned your students not being vulnerable. I'm hoping that you've seen that if you just participate in the space with them, they'll show you who they are." (Remember when I mentioned Trevor Taylor and his mic drop moment on the podcast: students are waiting on you to take that first step in being vulnerable.)

We show that we care by getting down into our students' spaces with them, by getting out from behind the desk or onto the floor and participating and listening to what we're asking them to do.

We have struggling teachers, but we also have good teachers. We have great teachers. We have outstanding teachers. And this is not just lip service. To show you what I mean, I think it's time for another quick activity.

Get out a sticky note or scratch paper or use your smartphone's notepad. Think about one outstanding teacher you know. Your most impactful educator. This could be a teacher you had as a student, a coach, or even a coworker. Keep that person in mind. What's the one thing that stands out about that educator that helped you and other students be successful? Don't make a bullet list; I want you to think deeper about this. Pick a word or phrase that describes that one thing and write it on your sticky note. Speak that word or phrase out loud. This graphic shows how other educators responded to this question the first time I did this activity.

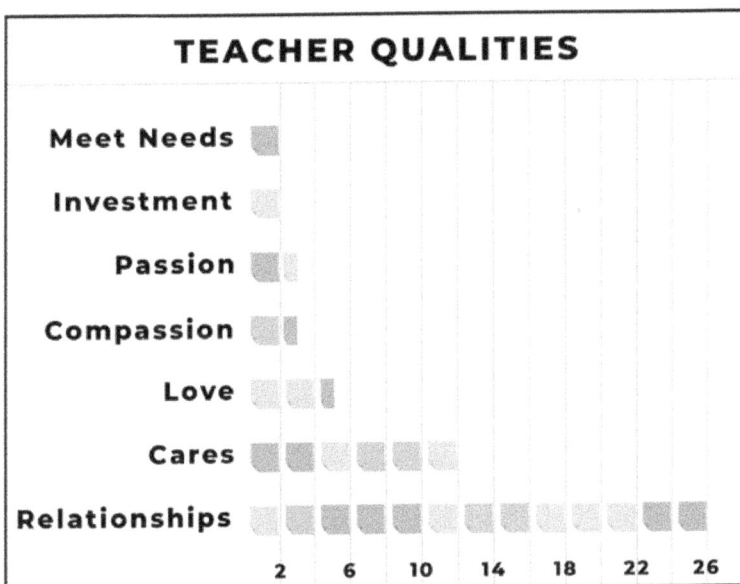

Some words and phrases are common. *Compassionate. Loving. Authentic. Caring. Relationships.* But you know what's not common? Words like *content* or *curriculum.* Very few educators say that when asked this question.

I'm not here to disparage content. But what this activity reveals repeatedly is that content knowledge or a curriculum lesson by itself is not what makes an outstanding teacher. What makes an outstanding educator is how that content is delivered. Excellence is not rooted in an educator's curriculum; it's rooted in their character, values, attributes, and mindsets. This is what we are striving for. But federal and state standards are pushing us toward content scores, which can hide our character from our students.

This activity is vital in addressing some of the blind spots within education. If you're a staff member conducting a book study on this topic, encourage each educator to develop their word or phrase and share it with your campus leader. Then, compile these responses to create a bulletin board or visual aid for reference. There will be moments throughout the school year when you may feel like you could be a better teacher. In those times, it's crucial to have a colleague guide you to this visual reminder: "What qualities did we define as an outstanding teacher?" Reflecting on these words can ground you and reinforce the idea that your worth as an educator isn't solely tied to your students' behavior or their assessment scores.

The Teacher's Keys

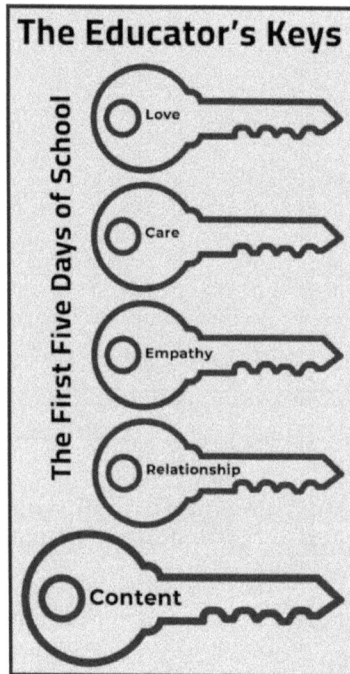

When we, as educators, first collect our keys of student success and put them on our classroom key ring, most of us expect to use the keys of relationship, empathy, and love. Then we actually get into the job, and content automatically becomes a big, heavy key on that ring, pushed by standards and mandates and what leadership identifies as important. Most schools create a similar pattern the first X number of days of the school year, we're told to focus on routines and relationships. Then the conversations change. How is our content? How are our scores? How is our test prep? Once that threshold of X number of days is reached, it's just content, scores, and outcomes. And those connection keys get smaller and smaller until they disappear.

If you've been in education long enough, you know how little importance those connection keys can seem to get when things get busy. If educational leaders solely focus on content, scores, and outcomes, the underlying message that gets conveyed is that relationships are not valued. When leadership doesn't focus on connections and hold us accountable for them, we can begin to question if we are wasting our time attempting to embed connections in the classroom.

What some educators do is drop the connection key in an attempt to handle all the rest. What outstanding teachers do is bring all the keys every single day. The full set. You teach content, and you relate, and you empathize, and you love.

We know connections are foundational in our classrooms. Connections provide the strength to keep going in every aspect of our lives. But if connections are so important, why are our legs so weak? How much lifting do we do with relationships? How many reps do we do throughout the year to intentionally build connections? We end up being very top-heavy in content and very weak in the knees.

Don't Be This Teacher!

Content

Relationships

Relationships are what make us successful. The content is fine, but if it doesn't have legs to stand on, it just topples over. I'm not saying make content lighter. I'm saying make the pillars of relationships stronger. Don't keep skipping leg day to work the arms of content.

We're looking for a balance. How can we use all our keys to deliver content *and* connection while not running ourselves into the ground or running out of time?

No significant learning can occur without a
significant relationship.
—Dr. James Comer

No educator should ever enter the classroom without James Comer's quote on their key ring. Without relationships, and the trust and goodwill that go along with them, content doesn't stick. Students don't even want to catch what we throw at them, let alone hold onto it. If standards require significant scores, we're going to need significant learning. But what we miss is that significant learning only occurs with significant relationships.

The current demands on teachers ask us to be top-heavy. And while education vaguely acknowledges relationships are important, there's not much support for teachers in doing that work. Administration and professional development tell you to build relationships, but *they don't tell you how*. Other initiatives or platforms may not explain how to effectively and appropriately cross-connect in the school setting. It's just expected to happen in the short time allotted to it.

It's not our fault we've been behind on building relationships. Educators have used the old playbook for so long that we haven't realized the game has changed.

Modernizing the Playbook

By far, our most impactful conference speakers are students. To paraphrase one high school student pleading with a thousand educators, "If you don't *connect* with me, why should I *content* with you? Because at the end of the day, I can go home and find out everything I need to know for this class on the internet." And this was way before ChatGPT or AI.

Creating connections is intentional. We need to modernize the school playbook to make them happen. Students are different today from the ones we were taught to teach. In the past, the model pupil came preprogrammed to hold more reverence and respect for educators, making them more likely to sit still, listen, believe, and behave appropriately. Students in the past were expected to repress their individuality—and to some extent, their emotions—while in the classroom.

In today's world, students can google answers to everything we ask and more. They can go on social media and see adults behaving like idiots, so they're not as likely to swallow whatever rule or idea educators throw at them, such as don't question adults or do what you are told to do the first time. They are now encouraged from a young age to speak up about what they don't like and to be individuals.

That's the difference the old playbook can't handle. Students are not shy to show you they don't trust you. They're told now they don't have to hide their needs and feelings of injustice. And these needs and values are compounded as the world gets more complex. This is one reason we're struggling.

Again, we must modernize our playbook. Some of us are still using the early 2000s edition. We're teaching under the assumption that we are the sole disseminators of knowledge, experts standing at the front of the classroom, masters to our apprentices. But the internet and streaming have made that moot. There is a ton of knowledge out there written by very smart people, many of them also educators, drifting in digital bits just waiting for people to google it. And modern students are masters of that universe.

But listen to what this student said again: "If you don't *connect* with me, why should I *content* with you?" She's telling you, "I want to connect. I want to learn from you, but you must connect with me first. If you don't, I'll just sit in the back of your class, do my reading and assignments, look stuff up on my own, get an A on your test, and never think about you again. Because I won't value you as a teacher. I won't see you. And I won't hear you."

Today, educators are facilitators and deliverers of information. They coach the acquisition of knowledge. We're no longer the sole experts and keepers of our content area. But we have one thing the internet, for all its facts, does not: the ability to relate. One on one, face to face, person to person. The internet, on its own, cannot value you. Cannot see you. Cannot hear you. You need a live person on the other end of the connection for that.

Relationships are the oxygen of human development. And what students are trying to do in the classroom is just breathe. They want to breathe in the modern-day air and understand that relationships are more important to them than ever. And it's not like relationships weren't important to us in school but we didn't have a voice or a choice of who to listen to. We were just told to "listen to your teacher" and, if you didn't like them, to suck it up. We didn't have alternatives. There wasn't a mindset that relationships were important for any point on that cross-connections relationship triangle—teacher, student, or student peers. If the goal was to help students keep up, the old playbooks left them behind.

Why do students disconnect? Why do educators get overwhelmed? Because it's rare that educators are taught how to build relationships and connect with students. Nobody gives educators permission to be ordinary. To not go a bazillion miles per hour on wobbly wheels. To not sacrifice their time and personal lives for their schools.

When things feel wobbly and dysregulated, it's okay to stop and to ramp up, revisit, review, and reteach our relationships and routines.

And it starts by being ordinary.

Be Ordinary to Be Outstanding, or Moments of Genuine Connection

On my podcast, a high school teacher who speaks and writes about education, Dave Stewart Jr., explains a concept that he calls "moments of genuine connection," which happens to be what our TCT tools try to create. [7] I love this concept because it gives educators a break. A big hurdle in building relationships is the time it often takes, and educators are strapped for time already. Dave reminds us that connections can be built in just small moments. I used the word *micro-frequencies* (not as shrewd, I know, but physics teacher here). Both terms imply you're chunking the relationship-building. You're doing so in little bursts, repeated day by day or week by week. Like drills in sports before you get to the big lesson. When you work with the TCT tools regularly, they don't take much time at all. Students quickly learn the drills and do them without much prompting.

Joe Beckman, cofounder of Till360, a powerful speaker at many schools and another guest on my podcast, says, "Teachers are asked to be too extraordinary." The flip side of this is educators are asked not to be vulnerable. Extraordinary people are expected to be invulnerable. Joe and I agreed *vulnerability* is a word many people don't like. It's like the word *moist*; it's squishy and gives you the heebie-jeebies. Joe and I wondered what could replace the word *vulnerable*. The answer? *Ordinary*.

When educators are pushed to be consistently extraordinary, they forget about being ordinary.

Your best moments of genuine connection come when you're just being ordinary, plain, old Mr. Curtis. They don't come when you're focused on being extraordinary and doing everything right. That's intimidating. What student wants to show their vulnerability

---

[7] Both podcasts can be found here:
https://www.listennotes.com/podcasts/relationship-centered-learning-kevin-curtis-bLgmK_7Gkqu/

to the eyes of perfection? Who can relate to someone who's superhuman?

Students buy into the teacher before they buy into the learning. To do that, students need to understand that we're real people with real lives. I can't tell you (and if you're a teacher, you know) how many times I've gone to a grocery store or restaurant and seen a student who, with eyes wide and mouth open, says reverently to their parent, "Oh! It's Mr. Curtis!" Meanwhile, I'm giving a panicked side-eye to my cart or table to make sure I don't have any incriminating tabloids or Grape Nuts or three empty margarita glasses. We're wondrous celebrity figures to our students. They think we live at the school, that we eat, sleep, and shower there. That we don't have families or responsibilities outside of that space.

It's powerful when students realize that we're human, just like them. We live in houses and apartments, just like them. We want to connect, just like them. But the other reason some educators don't include themselves when creating community in the classroom is because they don't know how. They are not naturally gifted at sharing, especially under these conditions.

So I asked Joe if he had a strategy for creating ordinary moments for connection. I'm all about the head, the heart, and the hands, so I wanted usable tools. Thankfully, he did. He recommended educators who don't know how to embed being ordinary into their classroom setting to intentionally take a pause during class once a week and share something from the FORD acronym: family, occupation, recreation, or dream.

That's simple enough. As we share intentionally with our students, we can take off the formal, untouchable, extraordinary educator and just say, "Hey, let me tell you something about my family." This doesn't seem like too big of a vulnerability. We don't have to reveal our deepest secrets or pain in any of these categories if we don't want to. And really, this is all we ask our students to start with anyway when sharing. We're just doing the same activity.

But even if you attempt to be ordinary and try the FORD strategy, the key is authenticity.

I experienced this firsthand. In our third year as a pilot at Ed White, we hired a new eighth-grade social studies teacher. Four weeks into the school year, he was struggling. My principal suggested I sit down and talk with him to hear how he thought he was doing. He admitted that he was struggling, and since we were focusing on connections, I asked him, "What do my students know about you?"

He replied, "Nothing! These are the worst kids I have ever taught."

I immediately sensed one of the main factors contributing to his struggles. My principal recommended that I spend an entire day in his classroom and help build a bridge to connect my students to this teacher. I knew there was not enough lumber to make this happen, but I am a good soldier and did as requested.

I had the teacher create a presentation where he could share personal information about himself with the students. Reflecting, I was following Joe's FORD formula without even knowing it. I was right. There wasn't enough wood to cover his robotic speech: "I have a dog. I like to do things outdoors." But the bridge building came to a halt during the third period.

Now, remember this was the third year I was the dad figure for all my students. We had built a relationship over those years; they had never seen me in a classroom like this. So they knew something was up.

"Why are you in here, Mr. Curtis?"

I responded, "What, I can't just come to hang out with you for a day?" Kids have a BR meter—a be real meter—that went off. I felt like I was on *Undercover Boss*, and my identity was questioned.

The teacher began his speech and went through the motions. Then, suddenly, one of my favorite students, LaJoy, shouted, "I know what you are doing in here. You are here because of him." She pointed to the teacher. Not wanting to be busted, I waved her off. She said, "You don't have to worry about him. We already figured out he won't last till the end of the year." Busted! They saw right through the scenario.

The sad part is that even after his attempt to share personally, he resigned a week later. The only thing I could do after that was recommend that we put LaJoy on the hiring committee for the teacher's replacement.

TCT tools rely heavily on sharing via talking but be careful not to fall back into wanting to be extraordinary and using talking as your measure of success. It's not about maximizing participation like in a content discussion. There's no test on this. There's no educator evaluation that checks off that everyone shared. The goal is to learn about each other and how we like to think and be in the world. It's to speak to students through their hearts and encourage them to be ordinary themselves and connect, not Johnny the Stoic Lord of the Back Corner, but Johnny Who Likes Hawaiian Pizza or, even more vulnerable, Johnny Who's ESL and Feels Embarrassed by His Accent. We want our students to know TCT activities have no ulterior motive, that we're not here to judge or embarrass them. These tools show that we are more alike than different.

So encourage students to talk, but don't make them. Don't say, "Johnny, you need to share with your group." If a student chooses not to talk, that's okay. There are tons of reasons a student might not want to talk in a small group. They're still participating by thinking about the question and listening to their classmates. They're still learning. And hopefully, they're also becoming more comfortable with their peers and us so that they'll eventually be able to share. No one wants to be pushed into the deep end when they don't know how to swim. Every student has their own developmental speed, even with connections. If you notice Johnny likes to listen and not talk, that observation is a win.

Maureen Palaoro, a successful educator for over thirty years, focuses on routines and relationships in her classrooms. "I think everybody in education knows students work better with structure," she told me. "But as we structure, we sometimes forget the importance of relationships." Her idea is also simple. When your class is dysregulated, your wheels are wobbling, and you're wondering what to do, first, stop. Revisit relationships. Connect with your students. Remind them you're all in this together. Taking that pause can re-regulate—get them back in the routine and the structure of learning. Dysregulation requires us to ramp up, revisit, and reteach relationships to reestablish routines (I warned you I like alliteration). It's an easy cycle to remember.

If you combine these philosophies, when things get wobbly and you stop, ramp up, revisit, and reteach your relationships, that's when you become ordinary (authentic) and share a FORD moment of genuine connection. Then you can reteach those routines. But as you're having your moment and creating connections, in CDC you are also cross-connecting. That's the perfect time to center your wheels and do a 60-Second Relate Break or 2-Minute Connection.

And once we learn each other's likes and dislikes, we can show we value, see, and hear our students throughout the day, in the ordinary moments outside of the TCT activities themselves. Maybe you learn a student is allergic to gluten, so the next time you have a class treat, you make sure to bring in a gluten-free option. Maybe you learn a student's mother is sick, so you do a quick check-in after class. Maybe you learn everyone is a fan of the latest Spider-Man movies, so you use that as a content example.

And that's what this is all about. Giving educators the opportunity to create real, authentic connections in the classroom. That's what we're looking for: ordinary moments of genuine cross-connection.

And these don't just happen. The best part about a tool is that we can plan how and when to use it.

Planning for Connections

I had an educator in Chicago ask me a very pointed question: "Do you want me to teach, or do you want me to build relationships?"

It made me pause. Why does it have to be one or the other? This is an unfortunate reality for most teachers. For some reason, some see these as two separate things that cannot exist in the same space. Eventually, I came up with a graphic to illustrate my discovery. And that discovery was the Three Cylinders of a Classroom Engine.

The Three Cylinders of an Educator Engine

Imagine your classroom as a powerful engine, with you as the driver. An engine typically has multiple cylinders that must all fire together to propel the vehicle efficiently and smoothly. Each cylinder represents a crucial aspect of classroom management, and your role in managing these cylinders is integral to the success of the classroom.

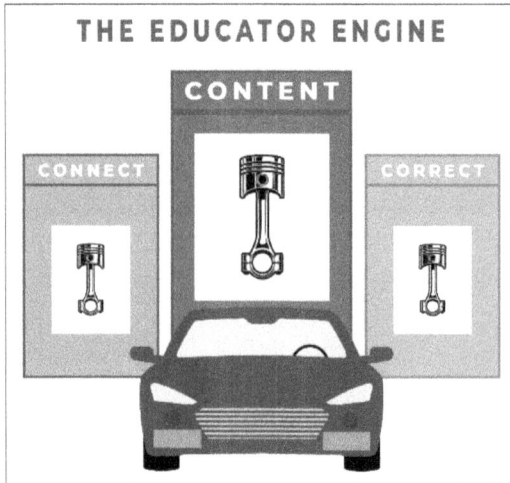

Content Cylinder: Delivers the academic material and ensures students are engaged and learning. Must have a plan to address educational needs and deficiencies. Content scores drive teacher evaluations and state accountability ratings, where we do most of our driving.

Correct Cylinder: Manages behavior, sets clear expectations, and uses various practices to address issues. Discipline referrals, tardies, and attendance are all addressed in this cylinder. State accountability in the areas of disproportionality and the school-to-prison pipeline has begun to take shape. Every teacher must create and maintain a classroom plan to address behavior.

Connect Cylinder: Builds and sustains relationships, creating a supportive and emotionally safe environment. There is no accountability for connections. There are no required plans to submit for connections. It is recommended but optional. Some don't drive with this cylinder engaged.

We treasure what we can measure.

—Margaret Hefferman

So as I reflected on the original question from the educator in Chicago, I started to observe how connection-driven teachers and campus leaders are accelerating past other teachers and campuses in the same building or district. Even if you don't know much about engines, you can see that a three-cylinder engine will run faster than most two-cylinder engines. But most of us are unaware that the connection cylinder is part of our educator engine. We rarely get professional learning on engaging that part of the engine. It's high time we establish requirements for educators to engage in professional learning, making them responsible for their own success.

All teachers must use the content cylinder and have a plan for content—lesson plans, activities, assignments, tests, rubrics. That's where most of the training and study happens. We know our pedagogy. We're prepared to teach this lesson in math. Most school leaders overemphasize this cylinder based on the weight of state accountability. It's the equivalent of consistently hearing we are not going fast enough.

All teachers must use the correct cylinder. All teachers are required to have a plan for correcting and managing behaviors. It's a basic plan, but we know what is and is not allowed regarding discipline and who we must contact depending on the situation. We're prepared to redirect behavior.

But how can teachers engage the connect cylinder? Is it reserved for times when the journey becomes challenging and progressing up the hill seems daunting? It's important to remember that this cylinder is suggested but optional. So as I observe and ask, "What traits do these teachers and campus leaders share that enable them to surpass others, as if they're cruising at a different speed?" I notice the common denominator is their consistent utilization of that third cylinder, the connect cylinder.

Everyone entering the field of education has the same three-cylinder educator engine. However, the power of the connect cylinder may have eluded you. You may have yet to be shown that this cylinder exists, or you may be on a campus that talks about the connect cylinder but never actually provides strategies to access it.

You see, I was guilty of this as a principal. I knew the value of creating connections in classrooms, but I fell prey to my superintendent's warnings that my state accountability scores, student engagement, attendance, and teacher retention must increase.

I was guilty of putting things like Every Kid, Every Day at the bottom of my email signature. Shouting, "Don't forget to connect with your kids!" as my staff was leaving a faculty meeting. It was an added thought more than a foundation. I missed this, and some of you might need to realize you have a third cylinder at your disposal. How many educators are only driving their class on two cylinders but have always wondered why others outperform them? Our foundational phrases, connect before content and connect before correct, illustrate the proper engaging of all three cylinders.

So how do we plan for connecting? I'm not talking about doing an activity or two but a real plan.

We're not prepared to set up a plan to cross-connect with our students. That's not something embedded into our preparation as educators because it's not required.

So here's what we do.

We're going to prepare a part of the lesson plan that is not only proactive but also practical, allowing you to embed it into your instruction time without adding extra hours. The reality is that these tools will add more to your plate, but with this practical approach, you'll be reassured and confident in your ability to manage your workload.

I have been guilty of saying things like the educator's plate is relationships, and all other things go onto that plate. Today, I am straightforward: the more we can learn to embed this into our instructional day, the easier it will be to digest a new way of doing things.

Remember our quote from earlier. Change is inevitable; growth is intentional. It will feel like you are first crossing your arms the other way, awkward and uncomfortable. But before you know it, with planning and practice at embedding, you will begin to feel more and more comfortable with having the TCT as part of your daily practices. That is why we have included our Connection Planner in the transformation process.

The Connection Planner is a simple way to proactively plan which tool will be embedded on which day of the week. So you are already preparing for content; now, you will have a planner to help you plan for connections.

Connection Planner

TOOL	Meet & Greet	60-Second Relate Break	2-Minute Connection	Positive Spark	Treatment Agreement & Relationship Goals
MONDAYS					
TUESDAYS					
WEDNESDAYS					
THURSDAYS					
FRIDAYS					

But what if you don't have anything proactively planned? Does the TCT still have value in your classroom in creating connections?

Absolutely! Once you have these tools in your toolkit, you can leverage those lost minutes of instruction, which I call the dead zone.

In these dead minutes between activities, or just after or before the bell, we often unplug and decompress, and our students hang there. And there's nothing wrong with that. But it's in the disconnect time that the least intentional learning occurs, and students are left to their own devices to learn relationship dos and don'ts from each other—which can have both positive and negative consequences. So how can we turn these two or three extra minutes from disconnect time into intentional connecting?

It's simple. All you need is a good question and a timer. Then, even if you didn't formally plan for that connection opportunity in your lesson plan, you can seize the opportunity when it presents itself. I recognize that we were never taught how to do this, and I am not going to act like I did it when I was teaching. "Hey, we've got two extra minutes. Let's do a 2-Minute Connection!" You have the tool; all you need is a good GTKY question ready to use. To get you started, we've included a whole chapter on criteria for good GTKY questions and how to generate them (Chapter 9).

When we build a weekly lesson plan, we can add an intentional TCT tool and GTKY question to that lesson plan. Maybe we put the tool in our two minutes of free time at the end of class. Maybe it's part of our attendance for the day. If you equate it to a workout or diet plan, it's the exact same thing: we're giving ourselves consistent instructions on what to prepare for and do at certain times all week. We're much happier and feel more in control of our physical and nutritional health. That's the power of proactively embedding a plan into your personal system.

It can seem like one more thing, but it's important. The most successful tools are used with some transparency, which means students know the tool's purpose and intended outcome (the what, the why, and the how). Once you teach the tool's purpose and how to do it, essentially front-loading the teaching, routines, and procedures for each tool, it will pay off on the back end, taking less and less time to implement the tool.

I have heard many school administrators say this over the years:

"Teaching should occur bell to bell." And what teachers hear is: "Content should take place bell to bell." That is a lot of pressure. I challenge our campus leaders and teachers to reframe the thought to "Learning can occur from bell to bell." Take the pressure off the classroom teachers to consistently teach some angle to the content at every moment.

I recognize that when I meet and greet students at the door, learning is occurring. I am learning the nonverbal cues and getting a pulse on my students' readiness for learning. We are still learning when we break away from the content and learn about each other.

For TCT tools that rely on conversation, set some classroom guidelines of what makes appropriate and civil conversation. Since I'm a sports guy, I frame this as what's "in bounds" or "out of bounds" in the game of classroom conversations. You may already do this if your content is discussion heavy. Guidelines should be established early in the year, maybe as your first GTKY question: "What makes for a good conversation?" or for littles, "How do you like to be talked to?" Give some dos and don'ts: "Wait for our friend to finish talking. Give everyone a chance to talk," or for high schoolers, remind them that we are only talking about school-appropriate subjects.

Enlisting students in setting the rules gets buy-in. Those are the rules they've agreed to, and they understand what they mean. Make a poster or chart and keep it in the classroom. Setting guidelines may take a few more minutes, but then you have those guidelines and can just gesture to them in all later conversations and discussions. Our Treatment Agreement tool is specifically geared toward expectation setting, though its scope is broader than just appropriate conversation.

Ideally, we'd all be those master planners: we'd have our tool and question written into our lesson plan for this day and time; we'd know its purpose; we'd even have a classroom conversation code of conduct. We'd be ready.

Some of us aren't always this prepared. Some of us will admit we didn't prepare a healthy meal plan but that we do need to eat better today—so we may get takeout that night but choose poké instead of pizza. For those of us a little less organized or more last-minute who suddenly think, *I need to keep to my healthy eating even if I didn't prepare a meal,* a minimal amount of planning goes a long way. Just have a go-to tool and a short list of questions so you're ready to go whenever those two minutes present themselves.

So when you review your plan for content, also review your plan for connection. If you see five Meet & Greets and two 60-Second Relate Breaks for the week, what do you need to make those happen? What are the activities for the Meet & Greets? What are the questions for the 60-Second Relate Breaks? The more you work in that prep, the more success you'll see from the tool because it won't come off as random or haphazard or—worse of all for a student—busy work. It will be an intentional, seamless part of the class.

One caution here as you engage the connection cylinder. Just like an exercise or diet plan, our connection plans have the exact same go-back-to-square-one consequences if we don't follow them consistently. Connection, like your health, takes constant maintenance. But over time, with habit, we realize just how much better we feel, how much healthier and productive we are, when we do it.

The big thing to take away from the planning is clarity. We already know how important it is to be clear in our expectations and instructions for content activities, both at an administration level and a classroom level. It's equally important to be clear about the connection between activities.

Now you have a connect plan to go along with your content and correct plans. You have all three cylinders running. The more you do in the connect zone, the more students will start to expect it, and the more smoothly it will go.

Conclusion

Once you recognize how the way you think about your students is preventing you from connecting to them in ways that are beneficial, you can change how you think about them and then how you approach them. We can go from great teachers to outstanding ones just by including ourselves in our connect cylinder activities.

Stress, conflict, and friction can always show up in the classroom—more so due to the lack of connections and other socioeconomic stressors. The world gets more complex all the time, and everyone in the classroom must adapt on the fly. Connecting helps us get to know each other, support each other, and give each other the grace and space to thrive despite it all.

But we can't do this with an outdated playbook. We must do some reimagining of the classroom here. Rewriting of the playbook.

Outstanding teachers show up with all the keys and use all three cylinders of the educator engine. They teach content; they manage behavior; they relate. We don't have to sacrifice our connection key at the expense of the content and behavior keys because the connection key is the key to the other two. Students are not going to trust and listen to us blindly anymore. We must give them something more than straight knowledge, something the internet can't: intentional connections.

We must connect first! If we connect more, we'll correct less. And when being in the content and correct cylinders becomes easier, we'll have even more time to connect.

But even starting out, when we feel there are fewer hours in the day than we need, there are always those lost minutes here and there at the start or end of class that we can structure around a TCT tool and a great GTKY question. Just two minutes, and we've added another layer of cross-connection to our classroom, reinforcing that sense of support and community.

The tools provided in the rest of this book are the kind that will help you get the results you are looking for from your students. They will give you the tools to create a connection-driven classroom. Look them over. Pick out your favorites, and plan to use them.

Part II
TCT for Schools

The Essential Foundation of Classroom Management

As we explore the transformative potential of the Connection-Driven Classroom, it is crucial to acknowledge an underlying truth: connections thrive in a structured environment. While fostering meaningful relationships is central to our approach, the effectiveness of these connections is contingent upon a well-managed classroom.

This brings us to a fundamental caveat: chaos combined with connections still equals chaos.

Chaos: The Multiplication Factor of Zero in Education

In any equation, the multiplication factor of zero results in zero, regardless of the other numbers involved. This principle also holds in educational environments: no matter how innovative or influential the strategies a school wishes to implement, **chaos multiplied by any factor—whether connections or content—will always equal zero.** Chaos acts as a kryptonite to successful schooling, undermining the effectiveness of all educational efforts.

The Devastating Impact of Chaos

Chaos in schools and classrooms is not just disruptive; it

fundamentally incapacitates the school's ability to function effectively. When chaos reigns, it consumes energy and attention that could otherwise be directed toward constructive educational practices. It creates an environment where:

- ✓ **Critical Components Struggle to Thrive**: Just as a garden choked by weeds struggles to produce, a chaotic classroom environment stifles the growth of essential educational components such as student engagement, effective teaching, and, most critically, the nurturing of connections that enhance learning and development.
- ✓ **Capacity for Proactivity Is Lost**: Educators overwhelmed by chaos find themselves in constant reactive mode, dealing with disruptions instead of focusing on proactive strategies like those advocated in the Connection-Driven Classroom. This constant firefighting leaves little room for implementing systems that could prevent issues before they arise.

Resetting the Equation

To combat the nullifying effect of chaos, schools must prioritize establishing a stable, orderly environment as the foundational step toward educational success. This involves:

- **Strengthening Classroom Management**: As Harry Wong highlighted, effective classroom management techniques that establish clear routines and expectations are essential. These practices help minimize disruptions and create a conducive learning environment, effectively resetting the classroom's equation to allow positive factors to influence the outcome.
- **Building Capacity for Connection**: With a stable climate, educators can shift their focus from merely managing behavior to actively fostering connections. This shift is crucial as it moves the school from survival

to growth and development, where meaningful relationships can flourish and drive educational success.

- **Empowering Educators**: Training and supporting educators to implement and sustain good classroom management practices empowers them to take control of their teaching environment. This empowerment is crucial for educators to feel capable of introducing and sustaining proactive strategies like those in the Connection-Driven Classroom.

Understanding chaos as the multiplication factor of zero helps illuminate why foundational classroom management is not just an optional part of teaching but a critical prerequisite for any successful educational strategy. Schools can create a fertile ground for connections and content to thrive by addressing and controlling chaos, transforming potential zeroes into flourishing successes. As educators, our challenge and duty is to ensure that we are not multiplying our efforts by zero but instead adding and multiplying through structured, connection-driven approaches.

The Necessity of Structure and Preparation

Drawing on Harry Wong's enduring wisdom, particularly from his seminal work on classroom management, *The First Day of School: How to Be an Effective Teacher*, we recognize that successful teaching hinges on structure, preparation, and consistency.

Wong famously stated, "The number one problem in the classroom is not discipline; it is the lack of procedures and routines."[8] This insight is crucial for implementing the Connection-Driven Classroom. Wong underscores that effective teaching is not merely about managing misbehavior but establishing clear,

---

[8] Harry Wong - classroom management. Accessed July 25, 2024. https://www.cueroisd.org/cms/lib/TX50010845/Centricity/Domain/18/harry%20wong%20classroom%20management.pdf.

predictable procedures that students can rely on. This structured environment is the soil in which fruitful connections grow. Without it, the seeds of connection we plant are less likely to thrive, as chaos can stifle the growth of relationships.

Establishing a Structured Environment

A structured classroom environment, as advocated by Wong, ensures that:

- ✓ **Clear Expectations and Routines Are Set**: Effective classroom management begins with setting clear expectations and establishing consistent routines. In fact, they must be so clear they cannot be misunderstood. These routines help manage student behavior and create a sense of safety and predictability, which is essential for students to open up and engage meaningfully with peers and teachers.
- ✓ **The Classroom Is Prepared for Learning**: Just as a successful restaurant prepares the tables before guests arrive, a successful teacher prepares the classroom for students. This preparation involves organizing the physical space, planning the day's lessons, and being ready to engage students when they enter the classroom.
- ✓ **Teachers Are Ready to Teach, Not Just Discipline**: Wong stresses the importance of teachers being prepared to teach and focusing on learning, not just disciplining. All students learn differently. This readiness includes identifying what your students will need to be successful with the day's lesson, which helps minimize downtime and disruptions that can lead to behavioral issues. Think about your transitions and potential pitfalls from students not knowing what to do once they are required to participate.

Why Classroom Management Matters for Connection

With the foundational support of effective classroom management, efforts to build connections can be significantly improved. A chaotic environment detracts from the sense of community and trust necessary for effective connection-driven practices. In contrast, a well-managed classroom promotes an atmosphere where:

- ✓ **Students Are Emotionally Ready to Connect**: In a structured environment, students feel secure and are more likely to engage in activities that require emotional openness and vulnerability.
- ✓ **Teachers Can Focus on Relationships**: With routines in place, teachers can shift their focus from constantly managing behavior to fostering deeper relationships with and among their students.
- ✓ **Activities Are Executed Smoothly**: Connection-driven activities require a certain level of calm to be effective. Well-established routines ensure that these activities can be integrated seamlessly into the daily flow of the classroom.

Prioritizing Classroom Management

Educators must ensure their classroom management is robust to benefit from the Connection-Driven Classroom approach. This foundational stability allows for successful implementation of strategies designed to enhance relationships and community within the classroom. As Wong elucidates, preparation in classroom management is not just about maintaining order but is also creating fertile ground for relationships to grow and thrive. Therefore, we must commit to mastering effective classroom management to pave the way for deeper, more impactful connections that enhance educational outcomes and student well-being.

My real-life experience supporting teachers in the classroom with these tools is that if they attempt to create connections in the middle of chaos, they will blame the tool and fail to recognize that the chaotic classroom environment was what set the connections up to fail, not the tool.

However, while creating structure will provide a foundation for classroom management, there is another vital component for mitigating chaos: clarity.

Clarity: The Cornerstone of Effective Educational Systems

My motto, "We must lead with such clarity that misunderstanding is impossible," underscores the importance of clear, unambiguous communication and expectations within schools. Lack of clarity can significantly contribute to chaos, affecting every aspect of school life, from the overall campus climate to individual classroom management.

The Role of Clarity in Schools

Clarity in school processes, expectations, and communication is the linchpin for effective educational management and student success. Schools that fail to establish clear, understandable, and transparent systems often see this ambiguity as chaos. Here's how clarity impacts various aspects of the educational environment:

- ✓ **Clear Expectations Reduce Ambiguity**: When teachers, students, and parents clearly understand what is expected of them, there is less room for misinterpretation and error, which are often precursors to behavioral issues and disengagement.
- ✓ **Systematic Clarity Enhances Efficiency**: Clear systems, from administrative communication to daily classroom routines, enhance operational efficiency and create a more cohesive educational experience.

✓ **Clarity in Communication Fosters Trust**: Effective, clear, and consistent communication helps build trust among all stakeholders—students, teachers, and parents. Trust is critical in creating a supportive school culture that values transparency and open dialogue.

Implementing Clarity to Counter Chaos

To leverage clarity as a tool against chaos, schools must take deliberate steps to ensure that every aspect of the educational process is transparent and understandable. This involves:

✓ **Developing Clear Instructional Objectives**: Teachers should have crystal-clear objectives for their lessons and student behavior and interactions within the classroom. These objectives should be communicated regularly and reinforced through consistent practice.

✓ **Establishing Transparent Systems and Procedures**: Clear, well-documented procedures minimize confusion and streamline learning and administration from how students move about the school to how they turn in assignments.

✓ **Training Staff in Clear Communication**: Professional development for teachers and administrative staff should emphasize the importance of clear, direct communication. Role-playing scenarios and communication training can help staff hone their ability to convey information succinctly and effectively.

✓ **Engaging Students and Parents**: Regular, clear communication with parents and students about school policies and expectations and the reasoning behind them helps to create an environment of mutual understanding and cooperation.

Conclusion

Clarity is indeed king in the educational context. A school that champions clarity in all its dealings sets itself up for a healthy, positive, and productive atmosphere where chaos is minimized and genuine learning and connection can thrive. Schools can transform potentially chaotic environments into educational excellence and relational success models by prioritizing clarity in expectations, systems, and communication. As we move forward with the Connection-Driven Classroom, let us strive to be models of clarity, ensuring our vision, methods, and goals are so clear that they cannot be misunderstood, thus paving the way for a more focused, engaged, and connected school community.

Chapter 4

Tool #1: The Meet & Greet

MEET & GREET

Each student is warmly welcomed at the door, fostering connections and ensuring they are truly seen. Create a community where every learner feels acknowledged and ready to thrive. The Meet & Greet is more than an opening—it's the foundation for a classroom where every student can be SEEN!

A middle school coach who attended one of our training sessions took the Meet & Greet away as the tool he would implement (remember, we're just hoping you'll click with at least *one* tool here). When he welcomed his students into the classroom at the door, he added a high five and a "Let's go!" for every student.

Quickly, he saw a difference in how his class started off. His students were energized. They started giving the "Let's go!" back to him and to each other during class. It became a classroom cheer when a student gave a good answer. If the teacher forgot to say it, the students would call him on it, "Where's the 'Let's go'? That was a 'Let's go!' answer!'"

A simple addition to greeting students at the door before class created a whole classroom culture that pulled students and the teacher together as a team and added a whole other level of engagement. It ended up cross-connecting in ways this educator had never dreamed possible.

Just with a little audacity added to the "Howdy!"

The Meet & Greet is what you do when you welcome students at the bus or at the school or classroom door. The Meet & Greet is a great introduction to the TCT best practices and one of the simplest tools in our toolbox. It's also the one most of us already feel comfortable doing. It's already part of our routine. And if it isn't, the tool makes it easy to incorporate.

Every teacher hears that it is important to be at their classroom door every day, meeting and greeting their students as they come in. Maybe your school leaders even passed an edict, requiring the doorway greeting as part of your day. But again, they don't tell you *how* to do this. This can leave us wondering, "Why am I doing this when I could be using these precious minutes to prep content?"

We don't have too many hard stats in this book, but here's one we find interesting. A 2018 study published in the *Journal of Positive Behavior Interventions* looked at 203 students being taught in ten different classrooms. [OBJ] It found that when educators consistently greeted their students at the door upon arrival, disruptive behaviors like blurting out, distracting peers, and leaving assigned areas dropped by 9 percent. Student engagement increased by 20 percent, equating to one hour of on-task time over a five-hour instructional day. For a fifty-minute secondary school class, that's ten extra minutes. There's a lot that can be done in just ten minutes of focus time.

Californians for Justice, a statewide youth-powered organization geared toward creating healthier, more just, and vibrant schools, also conducted a study. [OBJ] They documented 175 student interactions with teachers and staff over the course of a school day. What they saw was eye-popping to us. Over that whole day, nearly one out of five students did not have a single teacher or staff member make eye contact or greet them by name.

Suddenly, the little daily gesture of the Meet & Greet looks a lot more important.

But you don't have to take just scholarly words for why to do Meet & Greets. We have plenty of educators telling us the purpose they see behind their Meet & Greets.

Why Do It?

Every student deserves to feel valued, seen, and heard! Meet-n-Greets allow educators the opportunity to welcome each of their students entering the learning environment with a genuine moment of connection. Meet-n-Greets happen at the door, and so do connections! Be the educator who sees all their students.

That first impression is where students make a snap decision of whether they're going to give you the benefit of the doubt. It gets that initial buy-in for relationships.

The Meet-n-Greet ensures you start each class period with a connection. It's the opening welcome—a quick, positive interaction—that sets the tone for the rest of the class period. For some students, it may be the first positive interaction they've had all day.

Meet-n-Greets also allow an educator to do a quick check-in on how their students are doing. It's like taking the emotional pulse of the class that day. Pulse taken, the educator may then be able to adapt lesson plans on the fly to accommodate the mood of the class or one student without calling a lot of attention to that accommodation. This quick check-in can prevent an altercation with a student in a negative mental state because it allows the teacher to become aware of it and adjust for and with this student.

The Meet-n-Greet can allow for responsive action versus reaction. A little strategically placed TLC early can set up the whole class for success later in the day and, over the long term, create a healthier and happier classroom culture by fostering a sense of routine caring and belonging. It offers friendship and reassurance that everything is okay in their classroom world, even if the outside world is not okay.

On a simpler note, Meet-n-Greets helps students see models of good social skills and practice these skills themselves in a low-stakes environment. For some students, such as those on the autism spectrum, this opportunity to observe and practice greeting people repeatedly is vital to getting along in the real world.

Finally, a Meet-n-Greet can also just provide directions on what to do next, a segue to the day's first content activity, "Hi! Come in!

Sit down and get started on the warmup exercise."

Cross-Connection Outcomes

As for all our tools, we intentionally design our Meet-n-Greet to cross-connect on all three sides of that triangle: student to student, student to teacher, teacher to student. You need all three connections to effectively get the outcome of healthy classroom connections. Below is how the Meet-n-Greet forms these connections:

- ✓ Connects students to students through observing other students participating in the Meet-n-Greet.
- ✓ Connects student to teacher through the student greeting the teacher back.
- ✓ Connects teacher to student through the teacher greeting the student.

Keep in mind it's not just using the tool once; it's using it consistently—in this case, daily—to maintain and reinforce those connections. Resist getting distracted by doing content work, talking to a colleague across the hall while your students file in, or fixing your door décor. This is your first, best chance to connect.

I wonder how many people I've
looked at all my life and never seen.
—John Steinbeck

Let's See It in Action

So how do you make a threshold Meet & Greet part of your routine? How are you doing it? What does it look like? What does it sound like?

How do you put the passion and purpose for learning into a

simple "hello？"

We use the acronym SEEN to make sure that every educator is seen at the door and every student feels seen at the door.

S is for smile. A frown may look cute on Grumpy Cat, but it can be intimidating when worn by adults, and often we're not even aware we're grimacing as we think about things other than the students in front of us. Smiling is the world's most powerful way to make students feel at ease and communicate, "I'm happy to see you!" One student told me if his teacher smiled when he came in, he knew they could get along.

"E" stands for eye contact. This gesture not only builds rapport but also communicates, "I see you, and right now, you're the most important person to me." While eye contact is powerful, it's essential to recognize that some students may feel uncomfortable making eye contact for various reasons, and it's important to respect that.

The second "E" represents engagement, the personal interaction between teacher and student. Engagement can range from simple gestures like a fist bump to more creative approaches where students can choose their preferred greeting. The crucial aspect is authenticity—being true to yourself. Genuine positive energy captures students' attention and motivates them to join in the greeting. It fosters excitement and enthusiasm for being in the classroom.

Finally, the N is for name. More specifically, using the students' names. One of the quickest ways for us to build a connection and rapport is by learning our students' names. And I'm not just talking about the ones on the roster but each student's preferred name and pronunciation. Some students like to go by their last name or middle name or a nickname. Sometimes they want you to use a name they've chosen for themselves. It may sound like a small thing, but allowing a student to own their name is a huge sign of respect. And don't feel bad if your memory takes a few repetitions to work. The Meet & Greet can even be your daily name practice until you get them down.

Using students' names just lends that much more individuality and personal touch to your Meet & Greets. We want our students to know they're not lost in a sea of faces. We value, see, and hear them and their responses. Their arrival is worthy of our attention. And we can be the one who notices every single student, even the ones who often go unnoticed or prefer not to be noticed. It's hard for a student to completely ignore you if they hear their name. In just hearing that name, they've engaged.

So here is how to do it:

1. Meet your students at the door.
2. Greet each student by being SEEN: smile, make eye contact, engage with positive energy and maybe a fun action, and use each student's name.
3. Repeat daily. Consistency with this tool is key.

Keep it personal, positive, and possibly fun. Those are the basics to keep in mind when doing a Meet & Greet.

Signs of Sustainability

You will notice at the end of each tool, we have included a Sign of Sustainability (SOS), which is part of our system of sustainability for CDC and educators to help ensure their classroom is built upon the concrete of connections.

The Differentiated Discipline team developed the SOS because we all know that educators have way too much going on day to day. In the ever-changing world of education, there is always something new each educator is expected to be doing. It takes time and repetition to build new habits, and to ensure educators are in the habit of building and sustaining relationships, we have developed Signs of Sustainability (SOS). Each tool has an SOS to ensure that CDC is sustainable over the year. The SOS serves dual purposes.

First, each SOS serves as a quick reference to remind educators either how to use the tool or what each tool is composed of. Whether it is a 60-Second Relate Break or the purpose of the Treatment Agreement, the SOS can serve as a quick reference point for educators to quickly recall each tool.

Second, the SOS serves as a visual call to action. We envision educators taking the SOS and intentionally placing them around their classrooms or near their desks. In case an educator falls out of the habit of using any of our relationship-building tools, the SOS can remind them to use the four proactive tools to help create and maintain connections throughout the year.

Be ...

MEET

S - Smile

E - Eye Contact

E - Engage

N - Name

... at the door!

Adaptations, Accommodations & Advice

We would like to say you should take the tools and wrap them around yourself and your students. In other words, make them fit your and your students' needs. For each tool, we will offer ways to adapt and accommodate and provide advice for implementation. Adaptations to the tool apply to all students. You can adapt to the environment and general classroom space. Accommodation applies to individual students and may differ from student to student. Advice offers guidance for educators putting the tools into action.

It is important to note that there is power in letting students take the lead and tell you how to best adapt or accommodate a tool to fit their needs. Once students are comfortable with a tool, you can encourage students to provide input about potential ways to change a tool for their benefit.

As long as you're hitting the broad strokes—the mindset, the purpose, the outcome, the basic steps—and you're hitting all three points of your cross-connections, adapt and accommodate away to what works best for you and your students. The fittest evolve and adapt to the situation at hand, and that's part of the point of our tools and how we constructed them.

Adaptations

- ✓ Play music and dance with their students as they enter the classroom.
- ✓ When students come in late, go over to meet them, or have a student greeter.
- ✓ Assign a student to do the Meet & Greet if you have something come up and you can't do it.
- ✓ Position yourself so that you can see in the classroom and be in the doorway.
- ✓ Lock the door and have students line up in the hallway so that they are not in the classroom unsupervised.

Accommodations

- ✓ If eye contact is not culturally appropriate for a student, honor it and don't force it.
- ✓ Use menus to allow students to choose the Meet-n-Greet that they are most comfortable with.
- ✓ Develop individual handshakes or interactions with students to build another layer of connection.

Advice

- ✓ Spend time upfront doing the Meet & Greet to gain more time later (the more time spent to connect, the less time needed to correct).
- ✓ If time is an issue, choose greetings that are simple and quick.
- ✓ For older students, use a variety of Meet & Greets so that students don't get tired of one.
- ✓ For PreK and Kinder students, pick a maximum of three options for engagement, and keep them the same.
- ✓ Meet, Greet, and Repeat.
- ✓ Make it part of your routine.
- ✓ Make sure to pronounce students' names correctly.
- ✓ Be aware that asking students "How are you doing?" could potentially lead to long answers at the door and slow down or stop the flow.
- ✓ We certainly don't want to advise educators to shut down a student in crisis. If it appears to be a situation that can't be addressed quickly, let them know that as soon as you've finished greeting everyone, you will get back to them, or have a student who can take over the Meet & Greet.
- ✓ Share with each student how excited you are to see them.
- ✓ The Meet & Greet is a moment of one-on-one time. It is the first chance to establish trust with students individually.

Some of these suggestions also might make you cringe. I know *I'd* feel awkward dancing with my students! Trust me, I do my Texas two-step with two left feet. So don't feel you have to go too far outside your comfort zone for this tool. Tailor it to what fits and feels right for you—maybe even something that shows off a bit of your own personality. Even if you are a shyer, quieter person, you can incorporate something shyer and quieter into your Meet & Greet, like having each student choose a popsicle stick with a daily affirmation or line of poetry on it that you then collect when you take roll.

Takeaway

If your class is so content-heavy or so short that you don't have time for any of the other tools in this book, the Meet & Greet may be your best option to create connections. It's time already set aside for making connections, so just keep that time dedicated to the connect gear and watch how far a simple daily "hello" can go.

As educators, we often find ourselves doing things out of compliance. At other times, we do things because we're committed. Hopefully, even if you've been doing doorway Meet & Greets out of compliance because leadership told you to, now you'll see the benefits of this activity and commit to doing it every day because you want to.

Up next is another simple tool that doesn't take much time: the 60-Second Relate Break.

Chapter 5

Tool #2: The 60-Second Relate Break

60-SECOND RELATE BREAK

An intentional brain break designed for educators and students to momentarily step away from content and experience intentional connections. This Turn and Talk activity is a dynamic, efficient tool that takes just 60 seconds. Watch the energy shift as minds refresh, connections strengthen, and a vibrant sense of community emerges.

I had a professional development coach when I trained with the Bureau of Education and Research. It was the only time I've been coached since owning my own consulting business. My coach said, "Kevin, your participants need to be more engaged with each other and less with you." Part of the circle process included cubes with fun, safe questions written on their sides that would jump-start conversations. We would roll out a cube; it would land on a question, and we would roll with it.

We had bought our own cubes for our training with GTKY questions on each side, but we needed more participation, so we put cubes in the middle of our participants 'tables. They were green cubes, our color for proactiveness. I said, "This is a Quick Connect. During the training, whenever a "Quick Connect" green circle pops up in the presentation, roll the cube. Then you and your shoulder partner answer that question in a conversation."

It worked great—so great that we added a partner behind you as an additional pairing. We added groups of four. I used a timer to keep them to one minute because we added so many. The routine of the Quick Connect became embedded in our presentations.

And then we figured, if it worked for educators, why not for students? Since the time of activities is such a barrier for educators, we renamed it the 60-Second Relate Break so users of the tool would know immediately how much time they'd need to do it.

This is how this tool was born.

The 60-Second Relate Break is a simple and easy-to-use tool, fit for beginners learning to crawl. It only needs two things: a good GTKY question and a timer.

Why Do It?

A 60-Second Relate Break is a dynamic activity in which students break away from the content and turn and talk to their nearby classmates for a timed 60 seconds while the teacher moves about the room, listening to the students' conversations. It is a structured ear-hustling activity that allows cross-connecting to occur effectively and efficiently in the classroom.

This is a low-pressure turn-and-talk activity that allows for interpersonal communication and social connection. It requires us to mentally and physically turn away from content and talk to each other. It's a low-pressure situation because the topic of conversation is not about content—everyone will know the answer. It's also low pressure because the students are talking to their neighbors, students they most likely already have some level of familiarity with.

Cross-Connection Outcomes

The 60-Second Relate Break:

✓ Connects student to student through group conversation.
✓ Connects student to teacher through the teacher listening to those conversations.
✓ Connects teacher to student through a final sharing by the teacher to the class.

The hardest outcome here is the second. When it's your turn as the educator to connect, devote time to this role. Don't check roll, pour a cup of coffee, or walk out of the classroom. For that one minute, it's your job to listen.

Let's See It in Action

You've reached the point in your daily lesson plan where you've scheduled this Connect Gear activity, or you realize you have a couple of spare minutes and want to fill it with some intentional connections. You've chosen this tool and have your good GTKY question ready. Now, to set up for success with the 60-Second Relate Break tool, walk your students through it.

The first time you try any tool, make sure you introduce the tool, explain why you are doing it, explain the students 'role, and explain the teacher's role.

When it is time for the activity, give the class a heads-up, and state the purpose of the activity: "Hey, we have a couple of spare minutes. It's time for a 60-Second Relate Break! This will give us a chance to take a break from math and learn about each other." "When I say 'go,' turn to two or three neighbors to form a group."

You can have them turn to any combo of neighbors around them, either behind, in front, or to the side. We suggest groups of no more than four to give everyone time to talk. This can be done with groups of two, but the point of this tool is to form cross-connections with more than one person.

Explain the students' role: "Once you're in your groups, take turns sharing your answer to the question with your group members. There' are no wrong answers." Explaining the students' role allows them to be genuine and not fear judgment or getting it "wrong."

Remind students of classroom conversation guidelines: "Keep your conversations school appropriate. Be civil." Hopefully, you've already set these guidelines (see Chapter 3) so students know what "appropriate" and "civil" look like in practice. If not, you'll have to explain it here, and the tool may take longer than sixty seconds.

Explain your role: "I'm just going to walk around and listen to the interesting things you're talking about. Please speak in normal voices so I can hear you; I want to learn about you too." If you don't explain your role, you might get that educator-dampening effect, where the students lower their voices and feel uncomfortable sharing because the educator is hovering, listening for the "right" answer. If you encounter a shyer group anyway, no worries; move on to the next group.

As a suggestion, if you write out the day's lesson objectives on the board before class, include the 60-Second Relate Break and its chosen GTKY question so students know it's coming and have time to think of answers. This also prepares you to hit the ground running.

Start the timer. Say, "Go!" It's useful here to project the timer so the class can see it.

Now walk around the room and listen to the students. Don't speak; just listen. I know this is hard since we talk most of the time as educators, and we want students to *know* when we get inspired by them. But it's good practice for us. When we talk, we stop listening to each other. When we stop listening, we stop learning from each other, and we end up derailing the connections the students are making with each other. If they ask you a question, toss it back to the group. You'll hear some great stuff. Take it slow. If you have a big class, you may not get to everyone in sixty seconds. That's okay. Just start on the other side of the room the next time.

Give a warning the time is about to be up so conversations can wrap up: "You've got ten seconds!"

"Time's up!" Lastly, the teacher shares their answer to the question with the class. Don't forget to include yourself in the community connections!

Capture the connection by acknowledging you valued what you

saw and heard: "Thank you all for sharing! I really enjoyed seeing everyone participate and hearing what everyone thinks about X. If you didn't feel comfortable sharing today or didn't get a chance to, that's okay. We can't wait to hear from you next time." Then segue to the next thing on the schedule.

All done! And feel free to follow up on things you learned. Maybe you need to check in with a student one on one. Maybe you now plan to find out about X, since that's what most of the class talked about.

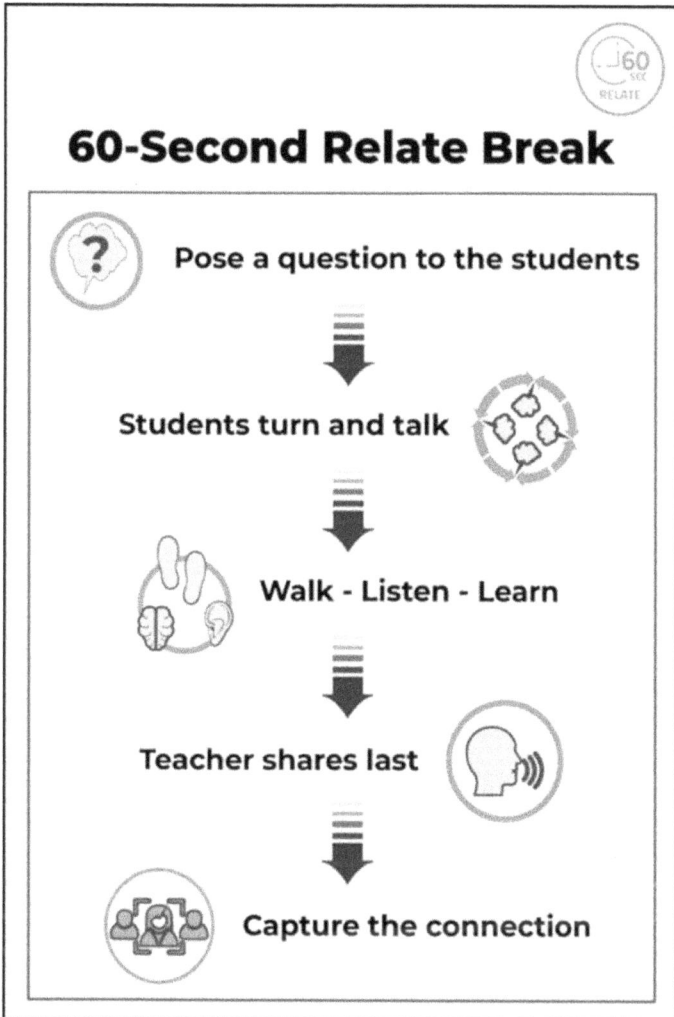

60-Second Relate Break

Pose a question to the students

Students turn and talk

Walk - Listen - Learn

Teacher shares last

Capture the connection

Adaptations, Accommodations & Advice

As you can for Tool #1, do for Tool #2: work with what's in front of you, and adapt and accommodate the 60-Second Relate Break as needed.

Whatever your adaptation or accommodation, always use a timer. Otherwise, it's easy for connecting to spill over into the time you've planned for content. As a football coach, I learned first-hand the power of the timer—a whole hour of practice planned to the minute, in five-minute periods, twelve in all. This is how you keep a 60-Second Relate Break from becoming a 3-minute Relate Break. It doesn't have to be fancy—your phone, a computer app, an old-fashioned egg timer—whatever lets you and your students know that the activity is over.

Generally, you can add to your pre-teaching the directive to keep talking in the groups even if they get done before the timer sounds. You can specify that these continued conversations can either gather more details about group members' answers or that conversations can drift into other topics, if they are school-appropriate. The goal of the activity is to prompt connection. If the students connect, it doesn't matter what they connect about.

Adaptations

- ✓ Shorten the time.
- ✓ Use it in small groups.
- ✓ Adding "and why" to the question encourages more sharing.
- ✓ Show a video or meme instead of just asking a question.
- ✓ Pair a question with an image.
- ✓ Shuffle the groups around with randomized group assignments so it's not always the same students talking to each other.
- ✓ Number students in order of sharing. Make the last student the one who may monopolize the time talking.

✓ If using "would you rather" questions, have students walk to one wall or the other to designate their responses.

✓ Consider having students write questions to ask the class.

✓ Incorporate a mindfulness exercise: two feet on the floor and take a deep breath before starting the conversation.

✓ Use a silent dialogue/silent sharing instead of a verbal one, where students pass a paper around the group and read and write responses. This also works in online chats or discussion groups.

✓ Use it virtually in chat rooms, breakout rooms or preset groups.

Accommodations

✓ Use visuals such as pictures and memes.

✓ Allow students to write or draw their answers.

✓ Allow students to have peer translators.

✓ If a student is not as confident in using the tool, make sure to pair them with a peer who can support them or a peer they trust.

Advice

✓ Have your SOS poster posted in the classroom and review before every tool.

✓ Use a timer to control time invested.

✓ Use at any point in the daily lesson: the beginning, before or after transitions, or at the end. Feel free to use this at different times with different classes.

✓ Beware of debatable, high-energy questions that can take your class off track.

✓ Make sure that you are not multitasking while you should be listening.

✓ Use raised hands or a nonverbal redirection to alert students to the end of the activity and bring conversions to a more organic close instead of shouting over student voices.

✓ Feature a student and spotlight their answer after the teacher's share-out.

✓ Use these at your staff meetings and PLC's. Adults can benefit from creating connections.

If you find an adaptation or accommodation that works, please share it with others. It may work for them too! And don't hesitate to get creative and graft another tool or activity you got from another workshop to this structure. The advantage of these tools is that they are endlessly adaptable but keep their essence. They provide good bones to build upon.

Takeaway

The 60-Second Relate Break is one of the quickest, simplest tools in this toolbox. As such, it is endlessly adaptable and useful for students at all grade levels. As a quick tool, it gets better the more you use it and students get used to its structure and cadence. It becomes a comfy routine and is a great tool to have in your back pocket when that surprise spare minute presents itself.

Up next is the 2-Minute Connection, a sibling to the 60-Second Relate Break.

Chapter 6

Tool #3: The 2-Minute Connection

2-MINUTE CONNECTION

An electrifying Stand and Share experience. In just two minutes, fuel intentional connections that extend beyond the classroom. Transform your classroom environment as you witness the power of creating connections. Elevate, connect, and let the magic unfold.

Like its younger sibling, the 60-Second Relate Break, the 2-Minute Connection only needs a timer and a few GTKY questions on hand. But, being an older sibling, it's a bit more mature and involved.

This is a stand-and-share activity, which means standing and speaking in front of the entire class, which can be more intimidating than just sitting and talking to a small group of neighbors.

Let me fill you in on how the 2-Minute Connection started. My band director at Ed White asked if I could come in and facilitate a version of this tool. Yes, this is one of our RD babies. In this case, it took the shape of a circle without the formal circle components. It was a once-around activity where one person stands in the middle of the circle and—you guessed it—shares and prompts others to connect.

Well, I said I'd facilitate for the band teacher, but I'd somehow missed how big band classes are. Fifty students stared at me in a big band hall, and I looked down at my talking piece and thought, "There's no way we'll get done in this forty-five-minute class. There's not even one minute per student, let alone two."

So how could I adapt this to a large group?

I put the talking piece in my back pocket and started to ask questions that related to me. The reason I say this is because it's good practice, as an adult in the classroom, to always lead by participating. For this tool, it's useful for students to have a model of what to do. It helps them buy in and dive in by getting some instruction and reassurance. They see us get into the pool first and realize it's safe, and now they know how to get in too.

The questions I needed to ask were shallow ones. I just wanted to step into the pool. In this case, I literally took a step into the circle and said, "My favorite color is blue. I had a blue room as a student. Who else's favorite color is blue?" After a moment, the students who also liked blue stepped into the circle. They didn't have to say anything, just communicate "I like the color blue too!" with that step. We pointed to each other and smiled, making a genuine connection.

Each time I asked for a connection, I got a response. "I like dogs. I have three Australian shepherds. Who else likes dogs?" and then "I like chocolate ice cream. My favorite brand is Blue Bell. Who else likes chocolate ice cream?" Some students stepped in repeatedly. They also liked dogs and chocolate ice cream.

Some started sharing verbally themselves, "I have a Rottweiler."

"My favorite brand is Ben and Jerry's."

Those repeaters strengthened their relationship with me every time they layered on a new connection. They were building capacity for more connections, adding strands of thread until the connection was as thick as yarn, as rope, among us. The students were braiding these strands of connection with their peers, too, as they saw those who also stepped in who liked blue, dogs, and chocolate ice cream.

Suddenly, we saw we were similar. It's important to note that similarity breeds empathy and compassion.

I upped the ante a bit. I was an experienced facilitator at this point, and the teacher had asked me to help build the classroom community, so I felt we could go a little deeper. With these questions, I stepped a little further into the center of the circle. "I grew up with one adult in the household. Who else has lived in a one-adult home?" The students looked at each other, and about a dozen stepped in. There was a longer pause as we saw each other. We maybe weren't expecting there'd be so many of us.

Then one student took another step toward the center. "I'm in foster care."

Before I got a chance to say anything, another student took a step across from him. "I'm in foster care too."

All of us in that space got to feel and see a rope form between those two students. Sometimes, if the sharing is deep enough, a strong connection forms right away.

After we closed the activity and I was gathering up my stuff to leave, the band director said, "I've had these students for almost two years. It's amazing how much we thought we knew each other. But today showed us we are more alike than we are different."

And that's the primary purpose of this tool: to help students and educators realize what they have in common.

The 2-Minute Connection has grown since then, and now has scaffolding options (the step-in as described above, using conversation cubes to ask the question, or asking an educator- or student-generated GTKY question), but the purpose remains the same.

Why Do It?

The 2-Minute Connection builds trusting relationships across an entire class by asking participants to share a bit of their personal life. This is to be used with a large group rather than a small one like the 60-Second Relate Break. It gives everyone an equal chance to engage with a request for connection from the teacher and other students. Like all our tools, the purpose is to offer a connection—in this case, one of recognition. "This is me; now who are you?"

It also gets a little deeper than our prior two tools. There's a little more vulnerability because of the unusual usage of classroom space, the larger group interactions, the standing (there's no desk to hide behind), and the extra time spent with each other. It may take a little more trust, and a few tries to see its best results.

Cross-Connection Outcomes

The 2-Minute Connection:

- ✓ Connects students to students through learning about each other through sharing and listening to each other's responses.
- ✓ Connects student to teacher through the teacher listening to each student respond.
- ✓ Connects teacher to student through the teacher authentically sharing their response to the question.

Let's See It in Action

Because the 2-Minute Connection is a bit more complex and can lead to the deep end of the pool rather quickly, there are a few tips we want to frame around this tool so your use of it will go more smoothly.

First, Don't Jump into a Circle.

While the 2-Minute Connection grew out of a traditional RD circle exercise, like the one you saw at the beginning of this chapter, we prefer you not jump into a circle formation when using this tool if you aren't yet trained in formal circle work or you feel confident you can smoothly get a floundering class out of the deep end without doing more harm than good.

Circles represent sacred practices to Indigenous tribes, and we want to respect that deep origin of meaning and practice and not use something without fully knowing what it is, what it does, and what it means to its creators. Remember, the original purpose of circle work is to unearth deep feelings and trauma that impact the community and then heal both the individual and the community through a long, slow, ritualized process. That is not what our tools for schools are meant to do. Hopefully, we'll work up to circles through more training, but it's best to walk before we run. And we also want to give students a visual clue as to when we're doing quick and shallow questions versus lengthy deep ones. Circles require more out of us, and students know this.

So instead of telling students to get into a circle, direct them to stand up around the classroom's edge. Everyone in the class stands in a square or rectangle or whatever shape your class space allows that's not a circle. Let the students stand and pick their spots first so you can mix up which students you stand next to each time you do this activity. It may help to stand next to students who are always engaged responders so they can get the momentum going right out of the gate.

On a side note, this tool gives the students an opportunity to get up and move. Simple movement and physical activity (e.g., standing at a desk, stretching) can boost students' mental sharpness. Research suggests that movement breaks can improve a student's ability to focus on a task for up to two hours.[9]

A benefit to getting the students up and moving to form a square or rectangle is that it helps fight the fatigue we feel from sitting too long without movement. When sitting, our bodies aren't burning as many calories as they would if we were standing or moving. Even a short period of sitting can lead to enhanced feelings of fatigue. In addition, if students have poor posture, they can feel heightened degrees of fatigue because poor posture leads to muscle tension and stiffness, which contributes to fatigue.[10]

Once everyone is standing around the room, introduce the 2-

---

[9] How Movement and Gestures Can Improve Student Learning—MindShift. "How Movement and Gestures Can Improve Student Learning—MindShift," June 29, 2021. https://www.kqed.org/mindshift/58051/how-movement-and-gestures-can-improve-student-learning.
[10] Axial Chairs. "Why Does Sitting Make Me Tired? | Doctor Explains How," March 28, 2022. https://axialchairs.com/why-sitting-make-me-tired.

Minute Connection so the students know its structure and what to prepare for. We want them to feel as comfortable and safe with this activity as possible if we're to get the trust and engagement that builds relationships. "We're going to stand and do an activity that lets us get to know each other and maybe discover what we have in common with each other. I'm going to pose a question to the class. When you have an answer, give me a thumbs-up. I will answer first. Then I'll point or motion to the next person so they know it's their turn. When it comes to you, your job is to give your answer. Keep your answers short—a few seconds—so we can get to everyone in the group. If it's not your turn, your job is to listen."

It's Important to Minimize Comments.

Social media has made us comment fiends, and some educators apply content gear techniques, like lengthy essay feedback, to the connect gear. As educators, we also have the idea that if we don't acknowledge or affirm what someone says, that person doesn't feel heard. We like to salt and pepper our students with those little side comments: "Nice work! I love that! Good job!" While there isn't necessarily anything wrong with this, these comments don't build relationships because they're just teacher-to-student. There's no input or offer from the student seeking this praise.

To create more cross-connection, students taught me an alternative way of commenting. Their feedback points out that students don't like the constant interruptions to the conversation or the educator's voice always being inserted into every action and interaction. They feel talked over. They feel the teacher's voice is more valued by the teacher than their own. They don't feel valued, seen, and heard when the teacher seems to always have the first and last word or always seeks to moralize or judge their actions and contributions.

Silent acknowledgment can be a powerful form of validation because you are allowing the speaker to keep center stage and maintain their own meaning of the sharing. There's no validation when the teacher says, "Good job!" but the students think their work wasn't done to their personal standard.

Silence can also diffuse energy when a student seeks center stage at the expense of relationship-building.

We have a great example of this recorded in a video we use at our training. In this class, one student acted as a timekeeper with a phone's stopwatch, and one student acted as the tally-keeper to note every time a new person spoke. Then the participants, including four adults, did their 2-Minute Connection, passing a mic around their space, with the students making up the GTKY questions. One question really got an engaged response: "What's a movie that makes you laugh?"

"*Home Alone.*"

"*Stepbrothers.*"

"*Hot Tub Time Machine.*"

"*Mama.* I know it's scary, but it always makes me laugh."

Then one student said, "*The Fault in Our Stars.*" This is a drama about a student dying of cancer. Not exactly a comedy. The student's response got a few gasps, "OMGs," and chuckles from his peers, but the assistant principal was right next to this student, and it was now the assistant principal's turn to go.

"*Ace Ventura, Pet Detective,*" and he passed the mic to the next person.

At the end, there were twenty-six responses in a minute and thirty-three seconds. It never felt rushed. It felt natural and organic—friendly. It stayed that way because neither the assistant principal nor any of the other adults made a big production out of the student who skirted the line of appropriateness or gave the student the spotlight he may have been testing for. Everyone trusted the process, respected the sharing, and treated every contribution with equal attention and affirmation—and left the value judgments at home.

This doesn't mean you can't check in with that student privately later, "Hey, I noticed you shared *The Fault in Our Stars*. That movie always makes me sad. I'm curious why it makes you laugh." The student might not even know. Some people feel uncomfortable when asked to reveal personal information, so they "act the clown" to cover that discomfort. If this is the answer here, you can always clarify that you'd much rather the student pass if they don't want to share instead of saying something that might distract other students or derail the conversation.

So instead of using a verbal acknowledgment when a student shares, try using a nonverbal, less intrusive one: a nod, jazz club finger-snapping, a smile with some eye contact. These techniques can be shared with the whole class to become part of the classroom culture.

Set Expectations for Behavior.

Like most of our tools, setting some ground rules for how to behave and treat each other in the classroom helps prevent any shenanigans that might distract, disrupt, or disrespect others while doing these activities.

Review any behavioral expectations or guidelines you want to see the class maintain during the activity: "We're not going to blurt out comments, talk over each other, or be sarcastic or a comedian. We're going to wait for our turn; listen to each other without comment; and be civil, kind, and honest."

If you need to speak to keep the flow of conversation moving and make sure everyone gets their time to share, that's fine, but keep those comments facilitating and not opinionated. Pair the observed behavior with its relational consequence to others. "Blurting things out isn't funny because it covers someone else's voice." In some of my own classes, I used the signal of one hand covering the other to signal we were covering someone's voice to keep the reminder subtle.

I saw a great example of using hand gestures to keep the activity moving from a fourth-grade teacher. She did a silent countdown with her fingers so the students could see. When the countdown ended, she'd say a quick, "Wrap it up," and draw a finger around her mouth. Or sometimes she'd offer, "We can always come back to you." It was gentle, and it didn't take the students' voices away; it just guided them.

If you want a more formal and comprehensive tool for setting behavioral expectations, see Chapter 8: The Treatment Agreement. But for now, just a quick discussion of what's appropriate to do while someone is sharing, and why doing these things is important to others, helps provide some guardrails.

Introduce your simple GTKY question. This will prime their minds for genuine response.

Let your students know that you will answer first to demonstrate what to do and model the appropriate length of response. AlSo let your students know the direction of sharing (to the right or left of you). I see too many educators just randomly call on students during this activity. This can create anxiety. When they don't know when it's going to be their turn, they can become anxious. When anxiety increases, sharing decreases. Giving them a direction increases a feeling of safety and security, even if they know when it's their turn.

Also let students know that if they need to take more time to think, it's okay to pass.

State the Question a Second Time.

Take a pause and give everyone time to think about the question and their answer. Direct them to show a ready response such as a thumbs-up when they are ready with an answer.

Remind students of nonverbal signals to help express connections to other students 'responses (e.g., snap fingers for an answer they like).

Let them know," If someone says your answer first, that's fine. You can have the same answer because we all might like or do the same things." They can also use the American Sign Language sign for "me too" to indicate they have the same answer.

As the teacher, you share first. The teacher takes the lead and answers the question. This breaks the ice and helps model what length and kind of answers are appropriate.

After you share, point or motion to the next person.

Allow each student to share their answer or pass if they need to.

Notice that the connection started with the teacher response, and it naturally returns to you when the person next to you ends the connection. This was very intentional when designing the structure. We, as educators, want to feel like we have most things under control in the classroom. When it comes back around to you, take a moment to capture the connection by highlighting that you learned something about them, they learned something about you, and they learned something about each other.

Thank Everyone for Sharing and Segue to the Next Task.

All done! If you have one student or a group of students with a lot of passes, check in with them privately: "What do you need to feel comfortable sharing? Do you need the question ahead of time? Do you need to go first? Last? Or is it something else?" And if the tool didn't make the connections like you'd hoped, always feel free to modify the way you do it next time.

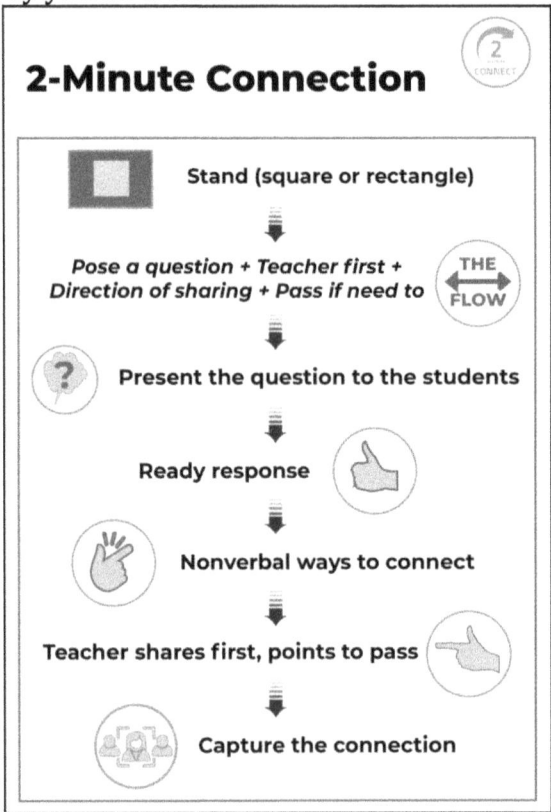

2-Minute Connection

Stand (square or rectangle)

Pose a question + Teacher first + Direction of sharing + Pass if need to | THE FLOW

Present the question to the students

Ready response

Nonverbal ways to connect

Teacher shares first, points to pass

Capture the connection

Adaptations, Accommodations & Advice

One educator at Ed White adapted the 2-Minute Connection: the students were asked to bring written responses to the GTKY questions. She did this because she wanted to give them time to be prepared and think about the question and their answer. She also didn't want any of her students to be influenced by peers' answers and fall into mimicry. If all her students said their favorite food was pizza, she wanted that to be authentic. She got a lot of thoughtful responses.

This teacher wasn't afraid to adapt the tools to fit her own class and account for her experience. She did what she felt was right for her and her students, and it worked. That's what we encourage any educator to do with our tools, including this one.

Adaptations

✓ Allow for more than two minutes the first or second time you and your students do the activity because of the explanation and instruction that goes along with it. Once the students know how to do it and have tried it out, then that two-minute mark should be easier to hit.

✓ Let students know that if they don't think they can be their best self (able to share and not be distracted or become a distraction), they can take the opportunity to move to another location.

✓ Implement a nonverbal signal for participants to remind others to "Check yourself" (e.g., a subtle signal as a reminder to focus on and listen to the speaker). Using it can teach self and peer accountability in a graceful way.

✓ Do this activity at the start of class, during a break between content lessons, or at the end of class.

✓ Mix up which direction you go each time you use the tool.

✓ Scaffold as needed using Step-Ins and Conversation Cubes.

- ✓ Conversation cubes can be used as a talking piece. It also allows the students to be able to read the question again.
- ✓ Project a timer on the screen/board.
- ✓ Post the question in advance. Have students write answers to share later.
- ✓ Have students put answers in a Google doc and show it to the whole class so that they can see all the answers. Ask if anyone wants to share or elaborate on their answer.
- ✓ Use it in an online discussion in a "chatterfall" format where each student types in their answer, and everyone pushes send at the same time, mimicking the cascade of a waterfall.
- ✓ Tell your kids that at the end, you'll open the floor for passersby if they need more time to think.
- ✓ Consider having students write questions to ask the class.
- ✓ Substitute the GTKY question with a more reflective prompt late in the week to help process the week's interactions. Prompts such as "Aha, Affirmation, Apology" work well, where students are prompted to share an aha moment in which they learned something exciting, an affirmation in which they got seconded on something they believed, or an apology to help repair a moment in which they made a mistake.

Accommodations

- ✓ Use individual nonverbal signals for students who may be oversharing.
- ✓ Have students write answers on a whiteboard and show their answers.
- ✓ Allow students to use an electronic device/app to translate their answers.
- ✓ Allow students to have peer translators.
- ✓ Allow students to draw their answers.

✓ Use visuals for students to point to their answers.

Advice

✓ Have your SOS poster posted in the classroom and review before every tool.

✓ Model a short answer so that your students know what length of answer you are expecting.

✓ Respond to inappropriate answers later to keep the sharing going (if it is not over the top).

✓ Provide something the students can fidget with while waiting to share. I love pipe cleaners! They are cheap, easy, and disposable. It's amazing to see the difference with and without something to occupy that nervous/exciting energy.

✓ Let students who struggle with sharing pick the question or have more thought time.

✓ Don't focus on passers.

✓ Structure and transitions are key! I would highly recommend placing dots or designated spots on the classroom floor that would clearly identify where students should stand to create the shared space in the classroom. This will assist tremendously in transitions as the students will clearly know where to go each time. Speaking of transitions, students release to the space by rows, tables, or colors. Control and clarity help reduce chaos!

✓ If the tool takes too long, instead of rushing, you can wrap it early, just be honest. "Looks like we'll need to close before we get to everyone. We'll come back to this activity later."

✓ Use these at your staff meetings and PLC's. Adults can benefit from creating connections.

While these adaptations, accommodations, and advice can be simple, the biggest ones may need to be improvised or even planned for the next iteration of your 2-Minute Connection because they address one of the major revelations of this tool: under sharing.

You're always going to have someone who overshares or under shares and breaks the flow. It's never going to go perfectly, and that's okay. Modeling problem-solving, flexibility, and grace is good for our students to see too. It lets them know they don't have to be perfect leaders and facilitators all the time either.

While oversharing can be handled with a gentle reminder of the activity expectations and structure, under sharing in the form of passing or distraction is the teacher's boogeyman here.

Passing happens, and passing can be contagious. If this happens, just take a pause and remind yourself you're not in the content gear right now; you're in the connect gear. This means everyone doesn't *need* to participate. You would like them to, and it would be more fun that way, but nobody *needs* to hear what Johnny's favorite ice cream flavor is. This is experiential and experimental, so just standing and listening is acceptable.

If you have a student who seems to be struggling with the appropriate way to make connections with any of the tools, go ahead and have an individual conversation with that student. What do they need to be successful? What will allow them to participate? What kind of accommodation, if any, are they open to? If you don't ask, you're guessing, and even a student who needs obvious accommodation will most likely want to check what that accommodation looks like, so they don't get singled out uncomfortably in front of their peers.

We're creating a safe space to share, and safety includes no force. It may be the only time during the school day the student feels no pressure to contribute. Maybe they want to revel in that release of pressure for a bit. Maybe they just don't know what to do. Maybe they think you, the teacher, are looking for a particular response, and they want to see other students go first so they know what the "right" response is. Or maybe they are so uncomfortable speaking in front of a big group that they can't speak at all.

Ed White had an Avid program that taught college readiness and study skills over three years, sixth through eighth grade. The teacher of that class used relationship-building tools, but it still took one girl in her class two years before she could speak in front of the entire group. When the student finally spoke during a TCT activity, the teacher cried.

And in the unthinkable scenario where everyone passes? Well, that's data. A lack of response is just as informative as a response.

It may mean the question didn't match the dynamics of the class, or it wasn't engaging, relevant, or understandable.

It may mean there's somebody in the room the class doesn't trust.

This happened in one classroom in which I did a similar activity to the 2-Minute Connection. Half the room spoke, and half the room passed. You could almost cut the room in half; the difference was that stark. As a consultant wanting to learn more, I went off script: "I notice this half of the room seems to want to share, and this half of the room seems to want to pass. I know the rules of the game say I'm supposed to just keep going, but I must ask: is there a reason?" Silence. "Well, we'll just keep going then."

After another couple of rounds, one student said, "Do you really want to know?"

"Yes. I'm just curious as to what's going on."

"Well, there's the cool students and the not-so-cool students. And the not cool students don't trust that whatever they say in here will stay in here, or they think that the cool students will make fun of them or judge them or say things about them outside of class."

Well, that elephant dropped into the middle of the room made me take stock of my perspective.

As educators, our job is not to judge students or to shame them. Our job is to understand them so that we can create cooperative communities where everybody feels like a contributor who is valued, seen, and heard.

If we're worried about students passing, we need to create a dynamic in the classroom where trust can happen.

This may mean going back to a tool that works with a small group that isn't so intimidating or revealing, like the 60-Second Relate Break, and really working to shuffle groups so it's not always the same students in the same part of the room.

That may mean easing into the 2-Minute Connection with a demo involving only volunteers in the center of the class while the rest of the class observes. You can even discuss those observations: what seemed to work well—and what didn't—to get people engaged?

That may mean we need to allow the students to drive the conversation. If the class is further along in their relationship with each other, has more trust, and consistently treats each other well, then it may be time to give them a bit more responsibility for those relationships. Let them come up with the questions, either prior to the activity so you can do the final selection or during. See Chapter 9 for more on this.

It may mean we need to give them the why—the reason we are doing this activity: "We're so busy learning material we haven't learned about each other outside this classroom. Learning about each other leads to treating each other better. Better treatment leads to more support. And more support means that when things get difficult, we don't have to face those challenges alone. We have a team who will help us get over our obstacles, whatever those may be, and be successful in this course." This is especially important for older students whose social relationships are already fraught with mistrust, judgment, and tribe-like affiliations.

I once went into a classroom cold. The students didn't know me or know I was coming. This was when we still used circles, and the teacher was doing an early form of CDC—just the RD community building. The circle had its circle rules: use a talking piece, respect what is said, don't talk out of turn, and the like. There were only four students. This was a discipline alternative education and placement campus, a.k.a. where the "challenging students" go, the ones who get caught with drugs or alcohol or weapons. In Texas, students enroll in a separate campus for thirty days or more while they do their time. It can feel a lot like jail. If they act right, they get to go back to their regular school, where they must reenroll, and the regular school often only gets about twenty-four hours' notice that the student is transferring back.

So I went in and sat down with this small group and their teacher. They asked if I'd model a circle for them, which in this case was just a less-developed version of the 2-Minute Connection. So we kept going around with questions, but the student to my right was pushing buttons. Testing. *What will happen if I keep blurting things out? Keep messing with the flow of the activity? Keep playing mind games with Mr. Curtis?*

It got to a point where I had to address it: "If you were going to act like this, why did you even join us?"

"Well," he said, "you didn't give me a choice."

Touché. I hadn't asked these students if they wanted to participate. He was pissing me off, but he was right.

"You're right," I admitted aloud. "So let's back up. Let's put our expectations out there." We pulled up the expectations on an overhead projector. I stated, "These are the group expectations. They apply to everyone, me included. If you would like to join the group in a conversation, these are the guidelines we will follow."

We sat down, but the two boys refused to join. So I said to them, "I'm going to have somebody come in to help you move to another space."

"You're just kicking us out!"

"No, I'm being clear here. By not joining us, you are saying you are not willing to meet these expectations, and I can't facilitate a healthy conversation without these expectations. You are making the choice not to be in this room because you can't follow these expectations. I'm not asking you to leave. You're welcome to stay. Just understand that these expectations don't change just because we're at an alternative campus."

So they left.

And the four of us who stayed had a profound conversation. One student admitted he was nervous to be going back to his home campus the next day. The scene of his mistake. But the other student with us, a young woman, said, "Hey, I felt the same way when I went back to my home campus the first time. You must trust yourself."

"What if I do the same thing?"

As I said, this discipline system feels like the juvenile justice system in its revolving door of recidivism. The students call their original campus "home," but it never really feels like home. There's no support and no conversation, and often, the students shuttle back and forth between the alternative campus and their home campus.

But I now know how to break the cycle.

"So who's going to support you when you get back?"

"I don't know."

"Do you have a teacher you really connect with at your home campus?"

"Ms. Green."

And the teacher who was part of our group said, "Oh, I know her." So she texted the other teacher, who was happy to agree to meet with this young man the next morning when he returned to campus.

This important, vulnerable conversation would never have happened if the other two young men had stayed with the group, wearing their resistance on their sleeves.

While most conversations in a classroom won't go as deep as this, there is still the option to allow students to sit out and quietly watch. Or if the student just truly can't deal with the CDC activity that day for whatever reason, it's okay to say, "If you let me know ahead of time, I can make space for you in another room while we do this 2-Minute Connection, and you can come back when we're done."

And just before you think, *"Well, then that student will always want to sit out or remove themselves",* keep in mind, they're willing to single themselves out in front of the whole class. If they are risking this judgment, then there's probably a reason, and they shouldn't feel pressured to stay.

We want to invite everyone to the pool party, not force them. If someone doesn't want to come to the party, then making them means it isn't a party anymore; it's a chore. It's our authority trumping their autonomy, and that sour mood will affect the entire space.

But if the heavily armored students can witness what we're doing, hear the fun questions, and see the clear expectations and how they work, they'll want to join. I've seen it happen more than once. Students standing on the outskirts of the class move to sitting on the floor just outside our space, and then they ask to be invited into the space so they can participate. Quietly, without comment, let them in when they're ready.

If you build a safe space and healthy community, they will come.

Takeaway

The 2-Minute Connection is a good tool to use to build a class-wide community among a large group. It works best once your class has gotten to know each other a little already. It's a nice progression to slightly deeper connections, and because of its unique usage of bodies in space, it can help wake a class up or nudge them out of a rut. Since it reveals similarities across the class, it's also a good tool to use to help reestablish connections when a class community seems to be drifting apart.

It's possible to use this tool when just starting out creating connections, but it may show the level of engagement you get. Remember, while I was new to the band teacher's group, she'd been teaching those same students for two years. They were used to playing music together. There was already a layer of trust to build on.

Everyone is different. Every class is different. Some may give you their heart on the first day. Others may need two years to even speak.

We don't like being vulnerable, exposing our soft underbelly to people who may attack it—make fun of us or judge us or invalidate us. Adults do this too. When I've done the 2-Minute Connection at training, sometimes the response (or should I say lack of response) is telling. One time early on, when we were developing the Step In 2-Minute Connection, I asked "Who likes country music?" I didn't step in (not recommended), and I saw one person do a half-step, realize they'd be the only one step in, and then reverse course. Now we know as the facilitator you always must ask questions that allow you to step in first.

We don't like being the only one. That's why, for this tool, leading by going first is so important. It's one of the glorious things—but also the most challenging things—about this tool: the willingness and trust to put yourself out there. For me, that's easy.

I've been practicing it for a long time. I no longer view vulnerability as weakness; it's just ordinary. But sharing ordinariness and getting in that pool first may be too much for others. And that's okay.

But if you can take that first step for your students, letting them see the ordinary can be a strength, too, they'll reward you with their connections. They're just waiting for us, seeing what we're willing to do for them, and they'll follow if we take that first step.

Our next tool is more straightforward than the 2-Minute Connection but no less inspirational: the Positive Spark.

Chapter 7

Tool #4: The Positive Spark

POSITIVE SPARK

An intentional burst of positivity between educators and students. With the help of this dynamic tool, educators create various positive interactions and experiences in their classrooms. It ignites your classroom into a thriving, connected environment, cultivating a culture that promotes increased engagement.

The Positive Spark wasn't even a tool until it happened in a fourth-grade classroom.

I think the assistant principal assumed the behaviors coming out of this classroom resulted from a lack of connection with the teacher in the classroom. I was contacted by the assistant principal to visit the campus. I was there to facilitate a community-building circle and discuss some of my observations with the assistant principal and teacher to identify the root issues driving challenging classroom behavior.

As we were starting to form our circle, I noticed four boys joined us later who were not part of the original class. I assumed they were coming from specials or rotations or maybe a pullout group. But they sat down and were ready to go, so I proceeded.

We began the circle with some GTKY questions. The kids seemed to be enjoying making connections with one another. I felt like I was co-facilitating with the assistant principal, who also joined us and helped guide the class space. But it felt like the conversation was getting stuck. It wasn't gaining any traction.

So I got direct: "All right, let's talk about the ways you treat each other in this classroom. Sometimes it's good; sometimes it's not so good. Have we talked about why that's happening?"

I asked the question again and allowed the students an opportunity to answer. But nothing came up that was obvious.

Then Bodie raised his hand. "I think I know what it is."

I asked, "What do you think it is?"

Bodie replied, "A negative spark. A negative spark is bigger than a positive spark, and a lot of times we're more negative than, we are positive."

Wow. I responded, "So what do you mean by that?"

Bodie said, "Mr. Curtis, it's the way we come into the classroom. When we first get here, we are more negative with each other. We're like, 'Get out of my way. You stop. You shut up.' And that negative spark is hard to overcome. So that's why I think we are the way we are."

Double wow. I asked, "So what would you say we would need to do?"

Bodie thought for a moment. "I think we would just need to be more positive when we come into the classroom."

Okay. I turned to one of the four boys who came in late. "Hey, Donovan, why don't we practice being positive? Do you think you could find somebody in this space to give a compliment to right now? To show us what a positive spark could look like?"

Now what I didn't know was that Donovan had some challenging behaviors. And I know I cold called him, which is something I advise not to do, but it felt like the right thing in that space. I could see the flash of fear on his face but then a quick nod of acceptance.

"Give it a try," I encouraged.

So Donovan turned and gave a compliment to his friend on the right. But then, unasked, he gave a compliment to the next person, and the next person, and the next person. Electricity ran through the room. It felt anticipatory but also uncertain. What was this peer, who could be ill behaved at times, going to say about each of them?

You could see as he gave each person a genuine, authentic compliment, the relief and then the awe that washed over them. Their whole-body language went from defensive to relaxed.

Donovan went around the whole room. And when he finished, I said, "Do y'all feel that?"

"Yeah!"

"Donovan, come over here." Now I have this fourth-grade boy standing next to me, just tall enough to reach my chest. "What Bodie taught us today was that a negative spark is bigger than a positive spark. But Donovan just showed us that a positive spark is way more powerful than a negative spark." Donovan stood there front and center, and just glowed.

"All right," I said, "what do we all need to do?"

"We need to be more positive with each other!" the class responded.

I continue to ask, "When should we do this? It sounds like we need to do it when we first come in."

"Yes!" the class resounded.

"Okay, so let's line up outside the door," I replied. Everybody walked out the door.

We took a piece of paper (the teacher would later make a poster of it) and wrote on it, "Be the Spark," and we put it on the door. And, like a motto hit by an athletic team before going onto the field, every person who reentered the classroom touched that sign to signal they were ready to be positive with others.

Then we practiced various ways to be positive, including compliments, affirmations, high fives, and games like thumb wrestling and rock paper scissors.

At the end of this improvised activity, the classroom community was entirely transformed from a tense, negative atmosphere to a more positive, safe space. The class committed to positive action within the first ninety seconds of class. No one wanted any more negative sparks taking hold of the classroom environment.

We called the action the 90-Second Spark back then, both for it happening within the first ninety seconds of class and because it only took ninety seconds (or less) to do. And So the Positive Spark was organically created by a fourth-grade class, led by two very different boys. And it turned into one of our most effective tools.

One wrinkle to this story that isn't so positive: I learned afterward that the reason those four boys were late was because the teacher had been apprehensive about having them participate in a community-building circle activity led by an outside consultant. She had requested the boys be removed.

It's a common impulse, especially when trust has been eroded through behavioral challenges and educators are still not sure what the CDC is. They don't want to show the less-than-stellar side of their classroom, especially to outsiders. None of us do. The assistant principal was the one who noticed the boys were absent and insisted they rejoin the group.

As teachers, administrators, and consultants, we must practice that Positive Spark too. We must assume the best in our students, even if they made mistakes the day before. Negative expectations can be big enough to overshadow positive ones, but positive expectations are way more powerful.

So every day, first thing, light that Positive Spark. You never know how bright it can be.

Why Do It?

Steve Harvey, the great TV personality and comedian, wrote in fourth grade that he wanted to be on a TV show. And his teacher belittled him for it: "You ever know anybody on TV? You're never gonna be on TV." Now, every single year, Harvey sends this teacher a big-screen TV so she can watch him.

That teacher could have crushed Harvey, but his dad said, "Don't let this define you. You must be something different."

The Spark is an action, but it hinges on words. Words have power. They can make or break somebody's day. When I was a freshman in high school, we used to have to give our report cards to our football coaches. Every six weeks, we had to show that report card. The students with A's, B's, and Cs would go to one side of the room and take a knee. The students with D's and Fs would go to the other side and get paddled.

On one of these report card days, Coach Tatum walked over to the A, B, and C side of the room where I' was standing, brought me forward, and asked my fellow student-athletes, "Why can't your grades be more like Curtis's ? " I didn't ask for this; I just worked hard. And I never really feared the paddle so much as I feared handing in poor grades. And in that moment in freshman year, Coach Tatum gave me positive motivation instead of a negative punishment. I viewed his words as instilling in me expectations of leadership and responsibility. I was a role model. I wasn't the smartest student, but I worked harder because I always wanted to hand in my best.

Instead of invalidating students, we need to try something different. If you're not sure what to say, say, "Whatever you wish your teacher would have said to you, say that."
—Hal Bowman

Words have weight and power. We all know the phrase "He's giving me a hard time" has completely different connotations than "He's having a hard time." How we think about and speak about our students plays into what kind of interactions we have with them. Are we lighting a negative spark or a positive one? Are we expecting the worst every day or the best?

Make things happen instead of waiting for things to happen. If you wait to address negative behaviors until after the fact, when they become habits, they are harder to overcome. So create a habit of positive behavior instead.

On a side note, some negative behaviors can stem from students being stressed. Why are students stressed out? This is a question with unlimited answers. Perhaps they're stressed because of things that are going on at home or in the neighborhood. Maybe students are stressed out because of stuff happening on the bus or in the hallway. Maybe students feel stressed by their peers in the classroom. Maybe you or your content stresses them out. Regardless of the reason, it would be beneficial for an educator to ponder what they could possibly do to help their students cope with the stress they are under.

According to Meteor Education, when it comes to reducing the stress students feel in the classroom, there are lots of things educators can do. Allowing for social interactions and keeping humor, fun, and laughter in the classroom are suggestions to help combat the ill effects stress has on student learning, and Positive Sparks can help ensure that happens with one easy tool.[11]

Many educators already encourage positive interactions in the classroom, and they may even have activities to practice them, but the Positive Spark makes this encouragement intentional and sustainable. Using it at the beginning of class helps set the tone and prevent negative feelings and behaviors from taking hold, because students and teachers intentionally start with positive momentum.

This tool sparks positive energy and sets expectations to allow for appreciation of everyone's unique personalities and gifts. There are many ways to appreciate, so there are a variety of ways to achieve this tool's outcomes. The important thing here, like with any of our tools, is to make this activity intentional and repeatable throughout the school year.

Cross-Connection Outcomes

The Positive Spark:

- ✓ Connects students to students through positive interactions with one another.
- ✓ Connects student to teacher through the student positive interactions with the teacher.

---

[11] MeTEOR Education. "Stress: How Teachers Can Help Their Students Cope," March 13, 2018. https://meteoreducation.com/stress-part-2/.

✓ Connects teacher to student through the teacher positive interactions with students.

Let's See It in Action

Sparks are built using different components: movement, positive touch, verbal interaction, nonverbal interaction, written, quote/meme videos/GIFs, and music. Incorporate and combine these components however you see fit—if you are spreading that positivity.

If you pick one component, we call it a Simple Spark. For example, your class needs a movement break, so you have the class dance for ninety seconds.

Other examples of Simple Sparks:

✓ Turn to your neighbor and say hello. (verbal interaction)
✓ Turn to a neighbor and give them a fist bump or air fist bump. (positive touch)
✓ Have the class say a positive quote or phrase together. (quote)

When you combine two or more components together, we call it a Super Spark. An example of a Super Spark would be to have everyone give each other high fives (positive touch) while the music plays (music).

Here are some other Sparks we've collected both online and from educators. There are hundreds, so don't feel like you have to use the ones we list here. Feel free to find and try your own.

Movement/Music Monday

Have the students enter the classroom with music or have the class create their own dance moves to create a positive learning environment.

Tabletop Tuesday

Small whiteboards are handed out to each student, and they write positive messages on them for other peers to read and receive.

Wonderful Wednesday

Find a peer on the opposite side of the room and affirm them by finishing the sentence stem, "You're wonderful because…" Have the students exchange the sentence stems.

Thumb Wrestle Thursday

If your school limits contact, this game can become rock paper scissors. The winner pays the challenger a compliment. By having the winner give the compliment, it becomes a way to teach students that it is not always about winning but about having fun and making connections in the classroom.

Staring is Caring Friday

This is a great example of a Super Spark because it involves verbal and nonverbal communication. Find a peer you've not Sparked with this week; invite them to a silent staring contest and see who smiles first.

The Affirmation Station

It's hard to give a compliment, but it's also hard to receive one. This activity does both.

Put two chairs in the middle of the classroom. These chairs are the Affirmation Station.

Put popsicle sticks with students 'names in a cup and randomly draw two to partner students together. Include sticks for the adults in the room if you really want to get all three cross-connections in.

Each student in the pair sits in one of the two chairs. Tell one student to give a compliment and the other to receive the compliment. Then switch. Let the students know they can use the appreciation sentence stems to form their compliment and response to the compliment.

Repeat this process for other student pairs until you hit your ninety seconds.

The Sticky-Note Spark

There are many ways we can give affirmations, and not all of them must be person to person or in a group.

Sticky notes are part of our school habitat. They are simple and made to be seen and often hold important reminders and messages.

Write compliments or affirmations on sticky notes and put them in students 'workbooks, on assignments that are being handed back, or hand them out before recess or dismissal.

You can also write notes offering words of acknowledgment and encouragement to individual students when you notice them struggling.

> *This year, I had my students write down what they wanted to hear on tough days. I collected those notes and handed them out when I saw students needed them. The power of their own positive words returning to them made a difference.*
> *—Danielle Sicotte, Teacher*

You can even have students put their own affirmations or words of encouragement on sticky notes and have them stick them on individual paper plates, each with a student's name written on it (make sure to include a plate with your name too!) or fill a cup or mailbox with them.

These notes could end up on a classroom poster and be used for other Spark activities. They could even travel outside of the classroom. In our presentations, we share one video example where one affirming sticky note traveled for a day from student to student, finally ending up with a custodian at the end.[12]

The Sticky-Note Spark is related to other types of positive signage, like yard signs, locker signs, or classroom posters that say, "I'm proud of you," or "Hang in there." But these signs can get disconnected from the person who put them up initially and lose their impact. It's much more powerful for a personalized note to go directly from one person to another.

This Sticky-Note Spark played out in my real life. When I was first starting my consulting business and traveled 50 to 120 days a year, my wife at the time decided to hide sticky notes throughout the clothes in my luggage for one of these trips. So as I went through the week, I'd find these little messages in my pockets. It was like an Easter egg hunt and produced that same feeling of quick joy in finding it. There's nothing to put a little pep in the step of a middle-aged man than finding "Don't forget I think you're hot" in the back pocket of a pair of jeans. Those notes gave us a connection even at a great distance.

When I told this story at a training, a group of five women got inspired. During lunch, they all texted their husbands that they were hot. They giddily showed me the responses they got.

One husband said, "Whatever you're eating for lunch, keep eating it. Can't wait to see you."

The next husband was more incredulous: "Was this meant for me?"

The third one, or should I say their teenage daughter who checked the text while the husband was driving, sent back, "Eww, Mom, stop talking to Dad that way," with an emoji throwing up.

The fourth text back was concise: "?"

The fifth read it but didn't respond. I told the woman he probably had analysis paralysis and needed more time to process.

These little positive Sparks didn't just change the trajectory of the husbands' days; giving these affirmations also changed the trajectory of this group of educators' days. They were excited and

---

[12] To see the video, check out: https://youtu.be/uxYNleF0JPo

delighted to see how someone they cared about received their compliment.

So take a pause for a moment in reading this book to send the first person who is topmost in your heart and mind right now a positive text—a compliment, an appreciation, an affirmation. If it's to your child, try using the sentence stem, "I'm proud of you because..."

You may get responses like:

"Are you okay?"

"What's this for?"

"Am I in trouble?"

Responses like this can be common. We're so busy we often don't reach out to affirm each other. We are not even expecting it, maybe especially from those closest to us. We are so starved socially for positivity that some people even initially think there's a hidden agenda to these compliments: if I say something positive to you, I expect something in return. It takes a lot of repetition and showing that this compliment is a gift, not a loan, for some to come around and accept the Spark.

Bucket Filling

There's a whole book on bucket filling titled *Have You Filled a Bucket Today?* but we've just borrowed the metaphor here.[13] A bucket filler is a kind, caring, and genuine person who wants to make someone feel good about themselves.

Actions and words could either be bucket fillers that made others feel good or bucket dippers that made others feel hurt. The system introduced a vocabulary for positive and negative interactions across an entire campus I visited.

This campus made literal buckets. They put cups in each pocket of a shoe organizer that hung on a door. These buckets (or in some cases, mailboxes) were not just found in the classrooms for

---

[13] McCloud, Carol. *Have You Filled a Bucket Today?: A Guide to Daily Happiness for Kids*. Ferne Press, 2006. https://doi.org/10.1604/9780978507510

students; one was in the teacher's lounge. Each bucket (cup) was filled with little notes of affirmation and encouragement. There was a system for everyone to contribute regularly to each other's buckets.

Staff Appreciation

Staff are like big students. We may be the adults in the room, but we like positive interactions too! It's great if the campus has a Big Spark plan for its big people on campus. I'm speaking to any school leaders reading this book now: don't forget to value, see and hear your adults too. Appreciation can feel disingenuous when it only takes the form of letting staff members wear jeans for a day. So remember to incorporate Big Sparks for the adults on campus.

One Spark that focuses on the school's adults is the Family Feast. The last Friday of every month, the school faculty, staff, and administrators eat together in a family-style get-together. Depending on your school's resources, this could be a potluck or donated or catered male, or maybe there's a budding chef on campus who likes to show off their barbecue skills. You can use the school grounds or cafeteria and have everyone pitch in however they are able to keep it affordable.

When I was an assistant principal, I asked my staff what would make them feel appreciated for the work they did, and they said, "Tea. And lemonade. So we can mix it." So I bought a self-agitating double punch bowl from a restaurant supply store, and every day the cafeteria staff filled one tank with iced tea and the other with lemonade and kept it stocked throughout the day. It was a Big Spark that the staff loved because they had access to this little indulgence all day long.

Another suggestion my staff had for me: don't just make handwritten notes; stop by in person. Notes can be powerful affirmations, but what's even better is in-person, unexpected Drive-By Affirmations. Stop by the classroom. Open the door, and go in. In front of the class, say, "Ms. Lisa, you rock. You're awesome. Your students love you. We love you on our campus. We appreciate all that you do."

The quickest and best way to know how to appreciate someone is to just ask them. Never in a million years would I have guessed the way to my staff's hearts was a public shoutout and an Arnold Palmer. I had to value, see, and hear my staff's wants to really make a difference in their day.

It doesn't take much to do something small to appreciate each other. Find out every staff member's birthday and favorite color. On each birthday, everyone on campus wears that color. When staff at Ed White started wearing each other's favorite colors for birthdays and their students found out about it, what did the students do? They wore birthday colors too! They wanted to participate, engage, and connect—all because the educators were modeling that for them. Sparks spark more Sparks.

Or have a rotating coffee crew. Who's bringing it this week? What flavor or brand will it be? It spreads the burden and adds a bit of mystery and anticipation to the week. Or everyone just knows each other's favorites and claims a morning to go down to the local coffee shop and hand-deliver the goods.

Adaptations, Accommodations & Advice

Adaptations

- ✓ Use as a nonacademic warmup.
- ✓ Post steps for the Spark on the board for students to follow.
- ✓ Have students assist in creating Sparks using their own ideas.
- ✓ Tell students what to do when they're done.
- ✓ Use music as a timer.
- ✓ Purposely pair partners or groups.
- ✓ Use various randomization techniques.
- ✓ Parent Pride: Assign some parent or guardian homework. What about your child's learning this year gave you the most pride? Share this homework with the students. If you worry about a parent not doing the homework, allow other adults special to the child to contribute.

Accommodations

- ✓ Use a timer to stay on track.
- ✓ Give options to participate.
- ✓ Provide clear and concise directions and expectations.
- ✓ Use visuals.
- ✓ Provide an opt-out space.
- ✓ Use word banks or sentence stems.

Advice

- ✓ Implement Spark Plans in the first ninety seconds of each class.
- ✓ Consider starting with Simple Sparks to help students get familiar and comfortable.
- ✓ Add an additional component to the Spark each day as a progression to a Super Spark.

- ✓ Check to make sure everyone has a partner or is in a group.
- ✓ Teach how to receive and give compliments.
- ✓ Use "backup" Sparks at other times during class in case the energy drops.
- ✓ Change Sparks up to keep them fun and fresh.
- ✓ Keep Spark Plans simple and consistent for younger students.
- ✓ Remember it is okay to have fun and be silly.
- ✓ Be yourself! Focus on your strengths.

Takeaway

Repeat your Positive Spark on a regular basis to keep that positive flame alive and embed affirmation and appreciation into your classroom. Your students will learn its process quickly, and later Sparks won't take as long as the first. You'll know it's embedded when even a substitute teacher can lead the tool successfully because your students already know what to do and want to do it.

If you introduce the Positive Spark in your classroom, like with all our tools, it works best when it's sustained and made systematic. When the connections it creates are reinforced and maintained.

Have you ever just wanted to be mad? One time I showed up mad to a meeting, and I just wanted to be mad. I've heard that the brain cannot be in two emotional spaces at the same time. And I have the experience to prove that it's true. One thing we try to do as an organization is to live what we preach and teach. We do Sparks at the beginning of all our meetings; it's embedded into our organizational culture. So I showed up mad and had to participate in a Spark. The Spark was to write a note or affirmation to each team member. Denise a.k.a. Circlemamma, reminded me that we *always* start with a Spark. She saw the state I was in, gave me a little of that "Circlemamma love," and directed me to a quiet space to write.

And as I took my moment, I had to tap into my heart and do this Spark. I started with my teams' names. Then I poured out my heart, and I' detested it because it' made me less mad with each pen stroke. Then I took my notes and put them in each person's cup—their bucket. I' was given my own and retreated to the corner like Gollum to look at all my positive, precious notes. And I didn't know how to be mad anymore. We joined back up as a team, loved each other a bit more, made everything work, and had a great meeting.

These tools are not just for the classroom; they're for life. Denise knew what to say when I was mad, and I was willing to go along with her lead because we'd already embedded the Positive Spark into our organizational culture. It was how we always started.

Have you ever seen a video in which adults in the school give positive affirmations to students? These videos were a faculty assignment given out by the administration. The adults on staff had to record a student receiving a positive affirmation from them. And you can see the students smiling. You can see the Spark take hold.

We must make the Spark sustainable. In this example, the principal backed it. Assigned it. In Donovan's case, it was the assistant principal who insisted he participate. But what if this backing doesn't exist? What do students hear off-camera? When do busy lives sideline the Positive Spark because we just don't think we have the time?

Spark interactions work best when they become organic, rooted in the classroom culture. Everyone hits that sign when they come in. Everyone shares the Spark without being told. Everyone commits. But students need some leadership and practice time before the Spark becomes a norm as part of their day.

Routine and consistency are important to maintain even when the school day is not routine. Do you still do a Positive Spark after a fire drill? Yes. Do you still do a Positive Spark after a behavioral incident? Yes. Do you still do a Positive Spark when there is a substitute? Yes. Do you still do a Positive Spark after a horrific global or local event? Most yes.

These are probably the most important times to use TCT tools because moments of upheaval can strain relationships, and if we don't immediately treat and heal that strain, it stretches until it snaps. You don't want to give the message to your students that when the chips are down, relationships don't really matter. You want to lead by example and show your students that yes, relationships *do* matter. How we treat each other matters. If you walk the walk, they'll follow you.

The key is don't stop walking.

And now on to our last, most complex, but maybe the most game-changing tool when it comes to compassionate interactions, the Treatment Agreement.

Chapter 8

Tool #5: The Treatment Agreement

TREATMENT AGREEMENT

A collaborative contract between students and educators. Craft positive norms for interactions, creating a powerful framework for a supportive learning environment. This robust tool guides redirection and reconnection, teaching the fundamental principle of treating others how they want to be treated.

One day, two years into Ed White's restorative discipline pilot program, I had a teacher ask me, "Has anyone ever not signed the Treatment Agreement before?"

"Not to my knowledge," I told her.

She replied, "Well, one of my students refused to sign this morning."

I let her know, "Okay, well, I'll talk to the student later."

I had a good relationship with this student already, so when I saw him at lunch, I asked, "Hey, I heard you didn't want to sign your class's Treatment Agreement."

"Yeah," he agreed.

"Is there a reason?" I asked.

"Mr. Curtis, that's a legally binding document, and I'm a minor," he said, and he walked off. Stunned, I was left wondering: did I just get played by a thirteen-year-old? And what could I do? A major part of restorative practices is that nothing is ever forced. You can invite inclusion and participation, but you can't force it. So what was my next move?

Well, if he'd played the "minor card," I'd play the "mom card." But by the time I called her, the wily student had already got to her first, and she was in full support of her son. "Mr. Curtis, I don't think my son should have to sign something he feels holds him accountable."

Quick as a cat, I reply, "Well, if your son can't sign, I'm going to need you to come down to the school to sign the agreement. It doesn't have to be now, but when you can."

Mom was now stunned, but she did come down to the school. I want you to picture standing in a classroom with me as assistant principal, the teacher, the student, and Mom in front of this handwritten Treatment Agreement poster with everyone's signature but this student's.

As I pointed to the relational categories of the agreement, I explained, "This is how other students are going to treat each other, including your son. Here are the expectations. Now, do you want others to give him his space when he needs it? Do you want them to not take his stuff without permission? Do you want them to speak kindly to him? Here is how students, including your son, are going to treat the teacher. Do you want students to respect her? Listen when she is speaking? Follow directions ? This is how the teacher is going to treat the students, including your son. Do you want her to know his name? Listen to him? Give him second chances?"

As I went on, Mom gave her son a side-eye, like, *I see what you tried to do here by giving me only part of the story.* I was getting through.

Then I went to the fourth category (this version had four relational categories), student to classroom. As I started to explain how students would treat their learning space, she held up a hand. "Stop right there." I stopped. "Where's the marker?" I gave her one. "Son, sign the thing."

Her son exclaimed, "But Mama, if I sign it, I have to do it!"

"Tyree Xander, what did I tell you? Sign this thing. Now, Mr.

Curtis, how do we get one of these things for the house?"

When I first learned of collaborative Treatment Agreements through the Institute of Restorative Justice and Restorative Dialogue, they were called Respect Agreements. We didn't want to use the word *respect* because that word carries heavier connotations than *treatment.* Like all of our tools, we've also made it more teacher-friendly over the years, but it still carries restorative DNA.

The Treatment Agreement is a contract collaboratively built between teachers and students. It sets expectations for how everyone in the classroom community will treat each other, and everyone agrees to abide by these obligations. According to Nancy Rey and Professor Douglas Fisher, both professors of educational leadership at San Diego State University, "When students mutually agree on behavioral guidelines, they develop a greater sense of ownership over the classroom."

Now don't get me wrong: this agreement does not replace classroom or school policies and rules. As educators, we're fans of rules. Rules bring consistency, structure, and safety. Rey and Fischer agree that "Classroom agreements are additions that uphold the rules and reflect the values of the classroom community."

As educators, we've all seen rules broken. We've experienced them being broken. It's almost as if being cussed out by a student is an informal rite of passage. Survive that, and you're now a full-fledged educator. And I'm betting if you have had that unfortunate experience, you didn't go home and dwell on the fact that the young man or young woman did not use kind words or school-appropriate language. It's that they disrespected and disheartened you.

Often, we get wrapped up in the rules and the breaking of rules. But it isn't the "no unkind language" rule we get hung up on; it's that the student directed that unkind language at us. After all the extra time and accommodations, we've given and all the sacrifices we've made to help them succeed, here they are, showing us the worst version of themselves. It's like they've wiped their muddy feet all over the relationship we've spent so much time weaving. All of a sudden, we don't feel valued, seen, or heard by the very students we've been trying so hard to value, see and hear. And that hurts.

So remember, it isn't the broken rule that preoccupies us; it's the broken heart.

The Treatment Agreement attempts to put the heart back into rules—for everyone.

Why Do It?

Like other restorative practices, the Treatment Agreement's main purpose is to prevent cracks in the classroom community's relationships and to repair relationships if they do break. It acts as the class's personal set of behavioral expectations.

Some educators think increasing familiarity by using the TCT tools can be a double-edged sword. Will students cease to respect my authority as a teacher? Will they feel they can get too personal? Will they start treating me like their therapist or their friend or their parents? But as long as we set expectations early and keep reminding students of our boundaries and the treatments we want in those student-to-teacher and teacher-to-student relationships, then we can maintain school-appropriate connections both in and outside the classroom.

Some educators we've talked to call the Treatment Agreement a game changer in terms of how they manage a class and redirect challenging behavior. If a student breaks a tenet of the agreement and treats someone poorly, it's easy to redirect that student, or even the whole class if there are multiple offenders, back to the Treatment Agreement. For some students, it only takes this reminder for behavior to change.

Why would students follow this agreement so willingly? Well, here's the key: this agreement is a representation of their needs and voices. Since students help make this agreement, buy-in from the students happens at the start. Unlike other class rules set down by authority figures, these are their rules to break. And they worked hard to come up with these rules. They understand these rules. They value these rules. And that ownership makes a difference for engagement.

It also sets age-appropriate behavioral expectations early so everyone is on page one on day one. It's a visual document every person in that class can refer back to when they fall short of those expectations. It may be the most labor-intensive tool we have, but it's also one that gets used every day, and most of this use is in the background. Students know they are expected to uphold the agreement in all their day-to-day interactions, and they know they'll be held accountable if they don't.

And on a simpler note, it introduces students to citizenship concepts like contracts, negotiations, compromise, and voting. And since the document they are practicing with directly affects their day-to-day life in the classroom, the stakes of participation and comprehension are more relevant. In other words, it's the best way for students to take these ideas to heart.

Cross-Connection Outcomes

A good Treatment Agreement is created organically and inclusively. It captures all the voices in the learning space: students, teachers, and teacher assistants or aides. By being a collaborative document, it automatically cross-connects.

The Treatment Agreement:

- ✓ Connects student to students through discussion about the tenets of the agreement and through following and maintaining the agreement.
- ✓ Connects student to teacher through discussion about the tenets, through the teacher writing student suggestions on an important class document, and through following and maintaining the agreement.
- ✓ Connects teacher to student through the teacher's contributions to the document and through following and maintaining the agreement.

The biggest hurdle to getting these outcomes is that maintenance piece. Live the agreement you make with your class; don't laminate it. The agreement as a piece of paper or digital form is not going to improve relationships; it's the use and practice of those tenets that seizes the day.

Let's See It in Action

On the front end, the Treatment Agreement takes some time to set up. It's a process to construct and takes critical thinking and participation from everyone involved because you have to unpack some meaning. Many educators who use one do it within the first week of a new class. This way, the amount of time they take up on that first day or week pays dividends until that course ends.

Here's the script:

Step 1: Introduce the Treatment Agreement

1. Give an overview of the purpose of the activity, something along the lines of, "The Treatment Agreement helps us set some classroom norms and expectations on how we're all going to treat each other with respect and kindness—student to student, student to teacher, and teacher to student."

2. Introduce the Treatment Agreement components to students. All these components together complete the agreement. The next steps walk you through how to do them.

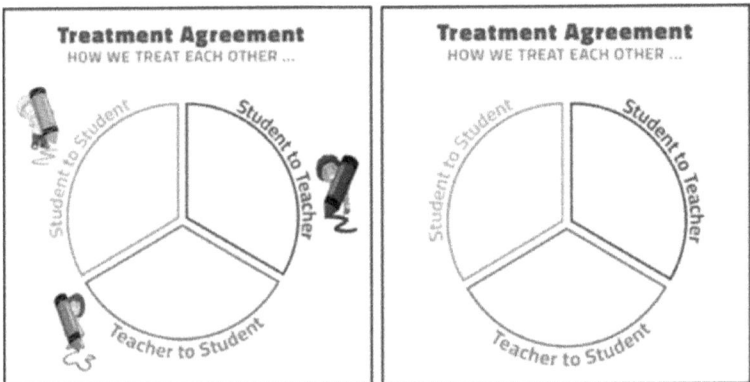

a. Wheel of Treatment: This Mercedes-Benz-like emblem asks everyone in the classroom—teacher(s), students, aides—to think about how they should treat each other student to student (S-S), student to teacher (S-T), and teacher to student (T-S). Make it a discussion. How are the interactions in each of these categories different? How are they the same?

b. Reconnect Rectangle : We all make mistakes. This concept makes a space for reconnecting when mistreatment occurs. Make it a discussion. What can we do to make up for mistakes or hurtful behavior? Or when we make it hard for others to learn and teach?

WHEN THIS DOESN'T HAPPEN, WE NEED TO RECONNECT BY ...

- Talking about it
- Apologizing
- Telling an adult
- Offering a hug
- Forgiving & forgetting
- Cooling down time or space

AND WE COMMIT TO A WEEKLY RELATIONSHIP GOAL.

WHEN THIS DOESN'T HAPPEN, WE NEED TO RECONNECT BY ...

- Giving me time to reflect
- Agreeing to disagree
- Genuinely apologizing
- Moving on and trying to forget
- Giving a second chance
- Accepting responsibility

AND WE COMMIT TO A WEEKLY RELATIONSHIP GOAL.

c. Relationships Goals: A commitment to continuous improvement in treatment areas the class struggles with and an acknowledgment of what we should keep doing.

Step 2: Identify How Individuals Want to Be Treated

Have everyone in the class identify what they think are the most important treatments for each relational category of the Treatment Wheel (S-S, S-T, T-S). This means teachers and teaching assistants too.

1. Have everyone in the class, adults included, fill out a Choice Sheet handout. You can have either physical or digital versions of these handouts. The Choice Sheet asks each collaborator to pick *two* treatments from each relational category on the Treatment Wheel (S-S, S-T, T-S) that are most important to them. Each category has a pre-populated list of ten common treatments we've identified from hundreds of real Treatment Agreements educators have shared with us. We have two Choice Sheet types: one geared for primary school and one for secondary school (see the handouts below). If your class is not yet able to do a lot of reading and writing see Adaptations, Accommodations & Advice below.
2. Once the Choice Sheets are filled out, collect them.

Step 3: Fill in the Treatment Agreement

On a whiteboard, big notepad, Google Doc, Jam Board, or some other physical or digital communal document, collect and show everyone's thoughts on how treatment needs to happen along with the Wheel of Treatment.

3. Collect the Choice Sheets and write down on your communal brainstorm document which treatments were picked for each category. No need to write down repeated choices, though some educators like to star or tally repeats to acknowledge each contributor's voice. Remember to include your own votes!

4. When all the choices are collected, discuss them. This makes sure interpretation and comprehension are aligned. Ask clarifying questions about these contributions—those *whats, hows,* and *whys*—to make sure everyone in the class agrees on what the treatment is, what it looks like in classroom practice, and why it is important. This process may change some minds about what treatments are most important, so don't just take a final top tally from the Choice Sheets; go on to vote on the choices.

5. You want to aim for about three to five treatments for each relational category to make the agreement comprehensive but manageable for everyone to remember and uphold, so everyone will now need to vote on their favorite treatments for each category (S-S, S-T, T-S). To tally the choices, you can:

    a. Take a hand raise, verbal, or written vote on each treatment option. You may want to make a rule like "You can only vote twice for each category" or "You can only vote six times total" to make sure the students prioritize, but this may not be necessary.

    b. If this is an online class, you can have students "like" options in discussion board threads or create a survey that they can fill out as homework.

6. From everyone's vote, identify the three to five top treatments for each relational category on the Wheel of Treatment.

7. Review the top choices with the class: "Are we all happy with these choices? Can we all follow these treatments? If not, why? What should be changed? Is there anything we should add? Is the wording clear, or should we revise or add a detail?"

8. Write the class's final choices of treatments on the class's official Treatment Agreement document such as anchor chart paper, flip charts, or poster board. You'll want to prominently display this document in the classroom or post it to your class's online course with other important course documents for reference later.

TREAT

Treatment Agreement Choice Sheet

In preparation for completing our classroom Treatment Agreement, look at the three relationship categories below (i.e., Student to Student, Student to Teacher, and Teacher to Student). Select the top two (2) treatments in each category that you feel are most important.

Students Treating Students

Help Me Clean Up

Be Kind

Share

Keep Hands & Feet to Self

Use Kind Words

Play with Others

Listen to Others

Ask to Borrow

Be Safe

Say "Hello"/Greet

Students Treating Teacher

Helping Me/
Helping Hands

Listen to
Teacher

Be Nice

Keep Hands &
Feet to Self

Raise Your Hand

Use Kind Voices

Tell the Truth

Take Care of
Supplies

Do Your
Best Work

Have Fun
Learning

Teacher Treating Students

Listen

Love Me

Be Nice

Smile

Be Patient

Help Me

Be Fair

Use Kind
Voice

Play with Us

Have Fun
Teaching

TREAT

Treatment Agreement Choice Sheet

In preparation for completing our classroom Treatment Agreement, look at the three relationship categories below (i.e., Student to Student, Student to Teacher, and Teacher to Student). Select the top two (2) treatments in each category that you feel are most important.

Students Treating Students

☐ Leave Drama at the Door

☐ Mind Your Own Business

☐ Honor Personal Boundaries

☐ Have a Positive Attitude

☐ Use My Name

☐ Appreciate Differences/ Accept Each Other

☐ Be Truthful

☐ Ask Permission to Borrow

☐ Listen When Someone Else Is Talking

☐ Encourage Each Other

Students Treating Teacher

☐ Give Attention

☐ Be an Active Listener

☐ Ask Before You Borrow

☐ Use a Positive Tone

☐ Be Open to Learning

☐ Actively Participate in Learning

☐ Let the Teacher Teach

☐ Talk in a Calm Voice

☐ Use School Appropriate Language

☐ Know I Make Mistakes Too

Teacher Treating Students

☐ Talk with Us

☐ Encourage Us

☐ Give Second Chances

☐ Fair and Equal Interactions

☐ Admit When You Make a Mistake

☐ Empathize with Us

☐ Listen to Both Sides of the Story

☐ Talk in a Calm Voice

☐ Don't Give Up on Me When I'm Having a Bad Day

☐ Ask How We Are Feeling / Doing

Step 4: Discuss the Reconnect Rectangle

The Reconnect Rectangle is to identify ways to reconnect after someone makes a mistake and breaks one of the treatments identified on the Treatment Agreement. Or maybe a mistreatment occurs that is not in the agreement but causes harm to an individual or the learning environment anyway. Say a student brings a lizard to class that scares someone and causes a huge class-wide distraction. Say we as educators unintentionally use words that are hurtful. How can these mistakes be made right?

L. R. Knost, author, social justice advocate, and founder and director of the children's rights advocacy consulting group Little Hearts, tells us, "In order for us to raise problem-solvers, we must focus on solutions, not retributions."[14] Focusing on solutions that "make it right" is what the Reconnect Rectangle aims to help us do. And yes, teachers and other adults in the classroom are held accountable to these solutions as well.

The biggest thing to remember with restorative solutions is that they give a chance to change behavior and provide the support and instruction to be able to make that change. They don't blame, shame, or maim someone for not knowing what they don't know.

Eric Jensen, author of *Teaching with Poverty in Mind* and *Engaging Students with Poverty in Mind*, introduces the "emotional keyboard."[15] If you imagine the keys on a keyboard, the middle keys are the hardwired human emotions: sadness, joy, disgust, anger, surprise, and fear. These are the emotions we're born with and can feel from the earliest ages. On the outer edges of the keyboard are the emotions we must be taught through experience and social interactions, things like humility, forgiveness, empathy, optimism, sympathy, patience, shame, compassion, and gratitude. But it takes

---

[14] http://www.littleheartsbooks.com/products-page/

[15] Jensen, Eric. *Teaching with Poverty in Mind: What Being Poor Does to Kids ' Brains and What Schools Can Do about It*, 2009.
Jensen, Eric. *Engaging Students with Poverty in Mind: Practical Strategies for Raising Achievement*, 2013.

a stable, safe environment to learn these outer keys of emotions. Students coming from poverty, in which survival is the only music they hear, are often not provided with as many opportunities to play with a full keyboard.

It's this emotional software that makes society a better place to live. But again, you must experience and see these emotions modeled by others before you can understand and practice them. And for some of our students, there are not a lot of opportunities to do this outside the classroom, so it's up to us to meet them where they' are and respond to their needs.

For example, maybe we have a student who wins a class race and celebrates by gloating, showboating, and otherwise displaying what we would view as poor sportsmanship. But if that's all the student sees outside of school and has never been shown sportsmanship, humility, and compassion, then that student also needs compassion and an opportunity to experience and learn something different. Also, as educators, we must be aware that we cannot expect students to exercise emotions they have never experienced before.

The Reconnect Rectangle is a great way to get this experience time for students.

From those same hundreds of preexisting Treatment Agreements, we've preselected the most effective reconnecting solutions for the Reconnect Rectangle. We did this because we noticed some classes that were inexperienced in restorative practices would fall into atonement and punishment, which further ostracizes and *dis*connects the student that made the mistake from the class.

The goal is to repair, not rupture further. Communicate, not confront. Mistreatments are mistakes, not crimes, and we want to help the person who made the mistake recognize it and get better at not making that mistake again. We get better by being able to recognize and hold ourselves accountable for our mistakes and by knowing how to repair the disconnect our mistake—the mistreatment—made.

To introduce the Reconnect Rectangle:

1. Share the list of pre-selected reconnecting solutions with the class.
2. Discuss the list. What does this solution mean? How might it look or sound when we practice it? Which solutions would work best for us and why? Which ones would be more difficult to use and why? Some examples include:
    a. I-statement sentence stems or templates for practicing reconnecting language. I-statements connect a feeling with an observed behavior or action: "I felt *scared* when you *brought the lizard to class,* " and "I'm sorry I made you feel *ashamed* when I *used words that were insensitive.*" We want to keep the focus on the behavior, separating the doer from the deed so the doer doesn't identify *as* the deed. We don't want students thinking, *"I'm a bad guy."* We want them to think, *"I made a poor choice, and it made my friend feel bad."* And we want them to feel empowered: *"But I'm still a good guy; I just made a mistake and need to do good things again."*

    I-statements also work great for the educator to redirect behavior by revisiting the agreement. "I'm confused" is one of my favorites. And I don't use it to call out students but call out behaviors. "I'm confused. I'm seeing some students getting out of their seats. I'm seeing some students get in each other's spaces. I'm hearing some side-talking." Follow it up with, "I'm curious: is this how we want to treat each other? Is this going to make us a more successful learning community? Do we have to add something else to our agreement? If I am holding up my end of the agreement, why am I seeing the students' end being dropped? What do we all have to say about this situation?"
    b. Apologizing. Now, we know that apologizing needs a behavior change to go along with it to be effective at reconnecting. But a sincere, genuine apology can help start someone on the path to improvement. It's good

to discuss just what a good apology looks and feels like and when's the best time to make it. A good template is: "I'm sorry for *bringing the lizard to class (behavior)*. It was wrong because *it scared you (the negative feeling or response it produced)*. I won't *bring any more animals to class (behavior)*. Please forgive me if you are able. Thank you for listening to me. How may I make amends?"

Once you've established what a good apology is, it may also benefit to discuss what an apology is *not*: something that is defensive and puts the blame back on the person who was mistreated, "I'm sorry, but your screaming made the lizard wiggle more," or "I'm sorry you misinterpreted what I said." There should be no *buts* in an apology.

It may be good to remind everyone in the class, us included, that we cannot control how someone else thinks or feels; we can only control how we respond to those thoughts and feelings. We can tell the other person we didn't mean to make them feel bad or that we did so out of ignorance, but that doesn't change that we've now caused the other person harm. We've ruptured the relationship, and now we have to repair it by attempting to reconnect by valuing, seeing, and hearing what they have to say.

c. One educator shared that she had students learn a nonverbal "check yourself" signal to try to prevent behavior from crossing the line into an altercation. When students started getting on each other's nerves and the mistreated student needed time to process, they'd give the hand signal. There were two warnings. If the behavior went unchanged, there was a third check mark on the chest to "check yourself," which meant the student doing the behavior had to take a pause and think about how to change tact at the moment. The educator reported students responded well to this reconnecting strategy, which promoted discrete communication instead of confrontation.

Step 5: Agree to the Full Treatment Agreement

Now that everyone is familiar with and has built all the components of the agreement, it's time for everyone to agree to abide by what y'all came up with. This is not always perfect (even the best educator can't); it's agreeing to uphold these treatments as best we can and making it right when we go up. It's about agreeing to a common language and criteria for accountability.

This step is simple: everyone in the classroom community signs the agreement.

There is rarely ever a refusal to agree at this point, but if there is, go back to #5 of Step 3 and probe the reluctance. If the person wants to discuss their concerns privately, you can accept a delay in their signature and work that issue out during a break or after class. You can even establish a provisional or trial period so the student can see the agreement working before they make that decision to sign. If you need to, you can call in administrative and parental/guardian support to help the student to see what the agreement is about and get it signed, like in the initial story in this chapter.

And if someone still refuses? Well, the majority prevails here, and if the rest of the class is good with it, those are still the treatments everyone will go by.

But again, the student who refuses is rare. It took two years for Ed White to find one. So don't go into this expected failure because its success rate hits it out of the park.

And if someone signs and breaks the agreement later? Well, you have your Reconnect Rectangle ready to go.

Step 6: Live the Agreement; Don't Laminate It

A completed and signed Treatment Agreement is a powerful tool for redirecting student behavior while keeping the relationship intact. Redirections tend to be more effective when utilizing the

Treatment Agreement due to the collaborative nature required to construct the Treatment Agreement.

Use the Treatment Agreement every day. If you don't, you might as well rip it up now because that's what the community will do to it if they are not reminded of it and held accountable for its treatments.

1. Revisit the agreement whenever someone new enters the classroom community. I've even heard some educators have student ambassadors who explain it when new teacher's aides or substitute teachers come in and have them sign it as well. This includes visiting parent helpers and community members! What better way to establish trust with your students than making sure everyone agrees to the treatments they decided on?

2. Redirect to the agreement when someone makes a mistake and causes harm to an individual or the class. Yes, that means pausing content for a moment, going to the Reconnect Rectangle solutions, and discussing mistreatment and what can be done to make it right. Remember, the Treatment Agreement also gives students permission to bring the mistreatments done by the teacher and other classroom adults up for reconnection.

   In a classroom in Fort Worth, Texas, as a teacher and I were speaking in a class, one of her students told the teacher, "Move."

   "My bad," the teacher responded and stepped us aside. The look on my face must have given away my shock at this less-than-tactful demand because the teacher quickly said, "Power of permission." We'd been standing in the way of the exercise the student needed to see on the board, and one of the class treatments was "Do not prevent me from learning." The student was in the right, though maybe "Give polite feedback" could be added to the agreement.

3. Aside from knowing how to solve mistreatments of individuals in the Reconnect Rectangle, it's also good to make the whole class aware that getting good at the Treatment Agreement is a process and takes practice. This

is where Relationship Goals come in. Every week, hyper-focus on a treatment to:

    a. Improve. What treatments are hard for us all to follow and why? What can we do to get better at these?

    b. Appreciate. What treatments do we all do well? How can we do more of this?

    c. Keep the goal prominent. Remind students it's the weekly focus. Nag if you must, so the behavior becomes rote.

4. Keep the agreement alive by updating it. This is one reason to keep the initial agreement to three to five treatments for each category, or about nine to fifteen in all. If you must go back and change a word or detail of a treatment or add a new treatment or a reconnect solution or goal as things, come up in the school year, you can.

Now pat yourself and your students on the back. You've just built a social agreement and allowed students control over their own treatment. This was the value, see, and hear master class!

Here are completed and blank Treatment Agreements for elementary and secondary students:

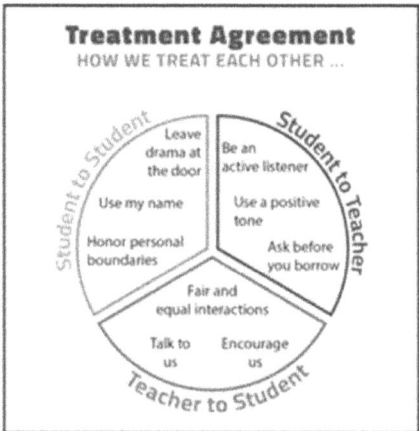

Adaptations, Accommodations & Advice

Again, we're not a program; we're a process. You don't have to wrap this big document around your class and be beholden to it; you wrap your class around it to make it work.

The Treatment Agreement, as one of our more complex tools, may need some changes to work with your class. This usually means finding ways to make it less confusing, especially for younger or special needs students, or even students who are just having trouble wrapping their heads around what you're asking for.

Adaptations

- ✓ Use online learning technologies like Google Forms, Jam Board, or Survey Monkey that can be populated with treatments identified by the Choice Sheets and allow students to vote. You could also vote remotely as homework to save class time.
- ✓ Break up or chunk the steps over a week, especially in a secondary classroom that may have only fifty minutes with students a day. Monday, introduce the Treatment Agreement and have students focus on the S-S category. Tuesday focuses on the S-T category. Wednesday focuses on the T-S category. Thursday focuses on the Reconnect Rectangle. Friday, complete it and sign it.
- ✓ Want to allow more student agency in the Choice Sheets but keep them efficient? Add a fill-in-the-blank line in addition to the ten choices given for students who really want to make it their own.
- ✓ Have students individually reflect on the Relationship Goal and how they can work to achieve it.
- ✓ Add a fourth quadrant to the Wheel of Treatment for self to self and discuss how student should treat themselves. Or add a quadrant for everyone to the classroom and discuss how to treat community spaces.
- ✓ For younger students, focus on one or two treatments, and then add to it as they demonstrate that they have learned the treatment.
- ✓ Have a student ambassador who explains the TA to new students, visitors to the class, and substitutes.

✓ For younger students who cannot read or write yet, break down each section to their level, and teach them what it would look and sound like before having them make their choices.

Accommodations

✓ Consider individualized Treatment Agreements for students requiring a more individualized, intensive degree of support.
✓ Consider handprints or fingerprints for students who are unable to write their names.
✓ Use visuals.

Advice

✓ Refer to the Treatment Agreement frequently.
✓ If working with multiple class periods/grade levels, consider one all-inclusive Treatment Agreement after construction.
✓ Review Relationship Goals at the end of the week or on Monday and determine goals for the next week.
✓ Revisit and revise as necessary.
✓ Describe how to use the Treatment Agreement in your substitute notes.
✓ Redirect by calling out behaviors; do not call out individuals. For example: "I'm confused because we are having side conversations, and we agreed that we would listen to each other."
✓ Teach your students how to respectfully hold you accountable.

We're sure you have other ways to adapt it to make it work for your situation and your students. If you keep those three cross-connection outcomes present and the agreement's main purpose in your mind, you'll have a document that builds and sustains relationships.

Takeaway

You can't reconnect a connection that wasn't there to begin with. The Treatment Agreement needs all its components to work well. The treatments in the Wheel of Treatment help identify the expectations for our relationships. The Reconnect Rectangle repairs these relationships when something goes sideways, and the Relationship Goals keep us striving to treat one another better.

It also works its best when other TCT tools are in consistent use and relationships have been built through the implementation of Meet & Greets, 60-Second Relate Breaks, 2-Minute Connections, and Positive Sparks. The connections we build with one another hold us accountable for how we treat each other. We have seen that when all the TCT tools are in play, everyone *wants* to follow the Treatment Agreement, and if something happens, they want to reconnect those connections.

This means, of course, that Treatment Agreements can be easier to use in primary schools where teachers have their students all day. Secondary schools can be trickier. Not every class period may require a Treatment Agreement. Or in some class periods, there may be more reminders of the treatments. This can lead to more interesting discussions about how to treat each other. Teenagers revolve around social relationships as part of their development, so this kind of discussion can be right up their alley.

If a school wants to implement Treatment Agreements more broadly and intentionally, it may start with gateway subjects like math or English—courses all students have to take. This will take school-wide buy-in and support from school leaders. With or without widespread support, you can still make a safe space in your individual classroom for fair and just treatment. Remember, it only takes one educator to make a difference to a student.

Yes, the Treatment Agreement is a mouthful of an activity to chew on, and it can be a bit scary to give up control, especially of the rules. Control is what we think keeps the chaos at bay, but it's not. This is demonstrated when one attempts to grip sand. The only way we can hold onto sand is if we cradle it, support it.

Trust your students to know how they want to be treated. They'll surprise you with their passion and wisdom. Even little students get the concept. I've heard of six-year-olds reminding each other, "Don't put yourself down; you can do it!" because one of their agreement treatments was, "Keep my and others' feelings and bodies safe." A little time taken on the front end made maintaining and redirecting behavior on the back end simpler and more communal. Quick, simple reminders took the place of longer teachable moments that could have presented bigger class interruptions.

A new teacher, only four years in, emailed us to share her experience using the Treatment Agreement. She'd been skeptical at first, as it sounded like a big ask, and she had just dialed in her content. But adding the Treatment Agreement had been a game changer. "I was able to remove my educator mask and just speak honestly about what I needed as an adult. And then hearing what my students needed from me. It was so profound and impactful. It's only a few weeks into the school year, and I can already see a difference in how my students treat each other."

When a mistake is made, it's a very freeing thing as an educator to point to a document students helped make that is written to their level to redirect behavior instead of meting out punishment for rules made by those in authority. You're no longer the rule enforcer; you're just the teacher. Just a fellow learner.

And that's the role all of us really want to play.

Chapter 9
GTKY Questions

As we said in Chapter 3, good GTKY questions help make a good plan of connection. Here's how to generate them.

What's a Good GTKY Question?

Ah, but wait: what *is* a good GTKY question? A good GTKY question makes a genuine, authentic connection and builds a genuine, authentic relationship. That means the question has to FESS up and be:

- ✓ **F**un
- ✓ **E**xtracurricular
- ✓ **S**imple
- ✓ **S**hallow

Fun is easy. Make the topic offbeat or unexpected or funny but also thought-provoking, something students want to answer that takes a bit more effort than just answering *yes* or *no* or *the color red*.

It also may help to come at the subject in a more off-beat way. Denise "Circlemamma" Holliday, was helping to facilitate a TCT tool when the teacher tried asking a question about bullying. No response. The topic was too serious and too big. But Denise quickly came in and added a bit of metaphor and a bit of fun: "If we had a vending machine like the ones in the cafeteria and this vending machine was filled with things that could help a bully stop bullying, what would be in it?" Then the floodgates opened.

Extracurricular means it's not related to content or academics. This is a hard one for educators. Resist the temptation to turn your "What's a topping that never goes on a pizza?" question into "Now if we divide the number of pizza slices by each person in the classroom, how many slices would each of us get?" That's an equation, not a connection, and it belongs in the content gear. If you don't believe me, trust your students. See how they drop their eyes and disengage when we turn connection into content. I know, we're wired for content, and that's how we're evaluated, but a little time *only* in the connect gear will make your time in the content gear more productive. In short, don't cross the gears.

If that's hard to do, ask, "Why are we using these tools"—to learn about math or English or to learn about each other?" If all we see of each other is through the lens of content—Jessi comes to class on time; Jessi raises her hand; Jessi answers questions; Jessi gets good grades—and vice versa—Mr. Curtis comes to class early; Mr. Curtis explains how to do the steps of a math problem; Mr. Curtis helps when I'm stuck on a problem; Mr. Curtis tells corny math jokes—then we only know each other as student and teacher. We don't know each other as people. Remember an educator's grocery store dilemma? Who are we outside the context of the classroom?

Extracurricular goes back to having questions that are not content driven. Don't try to teach with your questions. Base them on the hobbies or habits or activities you and your students like to do outside of school. You'll also want to keep inclusion in mind and make the question broad enough that everyone can answer. Not every student will play basketball or watch anime, but most will like some sort of extracurricular activity and watch TV.

Simple means the answer is short, sweet and opinion-based, though ideally more than one word. The question isn't going to trigger an essay, controversy, debate, or high-energy discussion. So it may not be appropriate to ask, "Tell us about your weekend," or "Who's the better basketball player, Michael Jordan or LeBron James?" or "Is a hot dog a sandwich?" because people have strong opinions on those topics and will defend them at length. "Who is your favorite sports player?" or "What was the last sandwich you ate?" is perfectly acceptable.

Be careful of questions that are *too* simple. "What's your favorite color?" or "What animal would you rather be, a cat or a dog?" only gets you a one-word answer the students don't have to think about, and it doesn't set up unique opportunities to relate to each other. A simple twist is "What's your favorite color to wear when you're happy?" or "Which animal would you be today and why?" These are still simple with brief answers but take a bit more thought and reveal a bit more about us. Even in a short TCT tool like the 60-Second Relate Break, it's okay to include *why* as part of the question. It keeps the conversion from stalling, and people want to naturally go there anyway to deepen the connection. There will be time to get it in. If not, it's not the end of the world. When you use the next tool, have the students that got skipped go first.

Simple expectations and structure also keep students from getting too hot or energetic. Some educators are afraid of connection time turning into a social free-for-all, but free-for-alls happen because the time is unstructured "free" time before or after class where anything goes. When students know the rules and how the game is played, they'll keep to them and expect accountability from the educator.

That brings us to the last criterion. In this case, **shallow** is good. We don't want to bring up deep personal confessions better left for the counselor. We know when this happens, the room will get quiet, and a heaviness settles over students and educators alike. The conversation stalls and we panic because there's nothing, we can do to resolve this issue in the span of two minutes at the end of class. So don't use prompts like, "Talk about a time when your first pet died," or "What's your biggest fear?" These will turn a quick group connection into group therapy.

If you're not sure your questions will lead to the deep end, run them past other educators or friends or family members for some perspective. They'll give you some indication of whether a question may head into the danger zone. You could even run them past your school counselors. It's their job to know the line between teaching and therapy.

Sometimes a seemingly innocent, high-quality question will get you into something heavy anyway. "What's your favorite meal?" could lead to "My grandmother's chicken-fried steak," or "My grandmother's chicken-fried steak, but she passed away last year, and I miss her." When this happens—and it will because questions can be refined, but they can't be foolproof—*don't freak out.* You heard; now just acknowledge you see and value this sharing: "That's good remembering of your grandmother, and I appreciate you sharing that with us."

Starting shallow doesn't always mean we stay shallow, but it does mean we want to wade out of the deep end by the end of the conversation. If an answer goes a bit deeper and feels like it's tipping into therapy and big emotions, there are a couple of things we can do. Pause the question and hold space for a moment before moving on to acknowledge the depth of the answer. Or make sure to wrap up with a funny/gross question, such as "Would you rather each a booger or worm?"

Shallow also means grade appropriate. It's at the depth your students can quickly understand and respond to. Middle school and upper elementary students love "would you rather" questions, such as, "Would you rather get bitten by a snake or run over by a rhinoceros?" I'd say "neither." And that"s okay. When you ask "would you rather" questions, there are five possible answers:

1. Option A
2. Option B
3. Both
4. Neither
5. An off-the-wall answer that elicits laughter from the group

We say all answers are okay if they are school appropriate. If it isn"t, address the student and send their answer later, as long as it is not too much out of bounds. If it is, discontinue the activity and follow your discipline plan, or redirect using the Treatment Agreement.

For kindergarten, simple questions, maybe with a graphic for them to choose from, work well. For a finance class in high school, we may squeak some content reflection questions in and ask, "What are you planning on doing with your money?" or "What's a big-ticket item you want to buy?"

Once you know how to FESS up, it's time to generate a bank of good questions so you never bounce a check-in because of insufficient fun.

How Do You Come Up with Good GTKY Questions?

If you want to bank some good GTKY questions, here's an activity. We call it Give Me Ten. Set a timer for five minutes and give me ten good Get To Know You Questions. You can use your own, your colleagues', or ones you find on the internet. Repeat this activity to get in the habit of collecting and using questions and to always have fresh ones in the bank. It's a great warmup or exit ticket for faculty meetings, grade-level meetings, or professional learning communities (PLCs) to add a good GTKY question to a communal document.

It's a great habit to practice finding or making GTKY questions throughout the school year for the entire faculty. Keeping questions fresh keeps the process of connection and using the TCT tools fresh. It keeps us participating, thinking and excited about these tools. And it keeps us from looking like old fogies in the classroom, which can happen quickly if questions include pop culture references. Ever ask a question about *The Matrix* and have your entire class stare at you blankly? Then you realize that movie came out in 1999, more than a decade before your students were born? And the movie that made you feel cool to watch when you were young now makes you feel like a dinosaur?

The simple solution is for school leaders to set up and keep up a communal document for the school, split by grade level, and have set events, like faculty meetings, where educators can share and contribute questions. It's also an opportunity to build capacity in question-crafting skills and make cross-connections among faculty members, who can share stories and give feedback on each other's questions. In this way, the questions never run out.

Keeping an active question bank also allows the questions to evolve along with the educators and their students and those connections. The shallower questions an educator asks at the beginning of the year may get a little deeper or more nuanced toward the end of the year when relationships are established. It's important that the complexity of the question also reflects the complexity of the connection, adding detail finishes and decoration to the house that's been built.

One thing that's fun to do as cross-connections deepen and students learn the structure of the questions we're asking is to include students in the brainstorming of GTKY questions. That could even be a GTKY question itself: "What Getting to Know You Question would you like to ask the class?" Have them turn in their answers and use the ones that fit the FESS-up criteria. Feel free to edit if the essential question is the same.

Yes, I know: the whole thing feels like taking the bumpers out of the bowling alley, but it's a great way to show students you see them growing into the relationship, too, and you trust them. They also get excited when their question is picked, and that validation creates a connection too. And, I'll admit, students are often better at asking GTKY questions than we are because they know what topics are at the top of their peers' minds. But the cherry on top is that if students are generating questions, *you don't have to.* This is something your students can contribute to the community. You can also collaborate with your team, departments, or PLCs. Developing questions during this time is an excellent opportunity to grow together in this process. Then you can become a facilitator of a bank of questions. Just pull, proofread, and plan. Work smarter, not harder.

Some of Our Favorite GTKY Questions

Of course, we're here to help you out too. So here' are some of our favorite GTKY questions we've collected from educators and the team over the years:

- ✓ If you had to have the neck of a giraffe or the trunk of an elephant, which would you choose?

- ✓ Would you rather have stinky breath or stinky feet?
- ✓ Would you rather always have a booger in your nose that moves when you breathe in and out or a piece of food stuck between your two front teeth?
- ✓ Do you prefer going to the movies or streaming movies from home?
- ✓ Would you rather own a dragon or be a dragon?
- ✓ What's your favorite animal?
- ✓ If you were a spy, what would your code name be?
- ✓ What's better: vanilla, strawberry, or chocolate milk?
- ✓ Would you rather live in outer space or at the bottom of the ocean?
- ✓ Would you rather be a superhero or a supervillain?
- ✓ If you could go to the moon, what one thing would you take with you?
- ✓ Would you rather have hairy arms or hairy legs?
- ✓ Would you rather be fast, strong, or smart?
- ✓ Would you rather have flamingo legs or T-rex arms?
- ✓ If you were a cereal, what kind would you be?
- ✓ If you could only eat one food for the rest of your life, which one would you choose?
- ✓ What would you rather have for a pet: a tiny hippo or a giant hamster?
- ✓ Would you rather bite your tongue or get a paper cut?
- ✓ Which is better: mashed potatoes or macaroni and cheese?
- ✓ Would you rather live in a fantasy or action movie?
- ✓ If you were given the option to live in a mansion for free and all bills were paid for, but you had to give up Wi-Fi for a year, would you take that opinion, or would you skip the chance?
- ✓ What is your favorite Disney or Pixar character?
- ✓ Would you rather swim with sharks or swim with alligators?
- ✓ Would you rather chew gum from under the desk or off the sidewalk?

✓ Would you rather be able to travel to the future or the past?

✓ Would you rather have one enormous eye or 200 itty-bitty eyes?

And now that you have a good idea of how to come up with the questions that fuel the tools, the last chapter answers some of the last-minute questions about the CDC you may have.

Conclusion

Believe

Now that you understand the current student mindset and the principles of the Connection-Driven Classroom, it's time to combine this knowledge with the five tools. This powerful combination will empower you to build stronger relationships with your students and enhance the overall health of your classroom community.

But what is the return on your investment? Our data shows that teachers who consistently embed these tools into their classrooms experience, on average, a fifty percent reduction in disruptive behaviors. Additionally, classroom teachers report increased student engagement, extended learning time, higher attendance rates, a safer classroom environment, and more positive home-school interactions. The focus on Cross-Connecting fosters increased trust, communication, and connections, allowing the classroom community to better understand and support each other. These benefits are not just theoretical; they are honest and achievable. They foster a sense of connection among classroom communities.

These tools have the power to transform our classrooms and our relationships. We cannot always see the cracks in our connections, but they are there, some wider than others. These hidden gaps represent our disconnection with each other. We will only treat each other better once we know more about each other and appreciate our similarities and differences. These tools help us build stronger connections with students. When used intentionally and consistently, students suddenly treat each other better, students treat teachers better, and teachers treat students better. The goal of these tools is to close those gaps! This work is about how we will be with each other in that space – the space that is not yet connected.

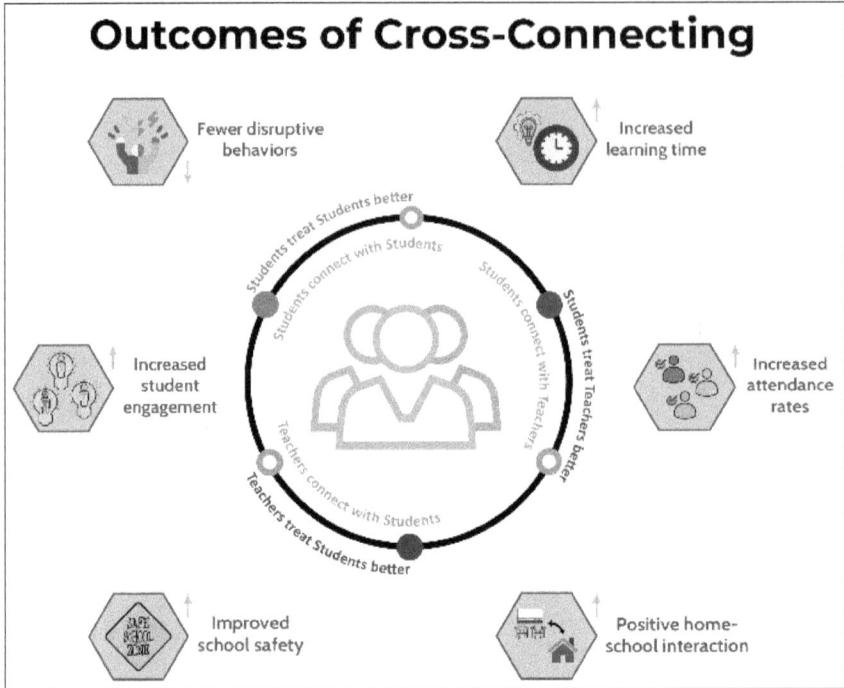

There is no math formula for success; there are only strategies and tools to help set you up for success. I'm not an expert. I'm experienced, and I gained my experience through screwing up over the last dozen or so years. I can give you adaptations, accommodations, and advice, but it doesn't mean you're going to be ready until you get in the classroom, roll up your sleeves, use these tools, and learn from your own mistakes. It's important that you don't give up once you start. If the tool falls flat, reflect, refine, and try another one. Many of our students are used to adults giving up. Don't let your fears prevent you from making connections in your classroom with your students.

We always say we focus on the process, not the product, but it's this success cycle that's the ultimate consequence of using the TCT tools consistently and intentionally. Don't get stuck on one student over talking, one student refusing to share, or even a whole activity flaming out. It's the accumulative effect, the layering of connections, that ultimately creates the relationships that get everyone through.

If we can give our students the grace and space to make mistakes, we can certainly give that to ourselves by setting ordinary expectations, especially in an area like relationships that is more social art than social skill.

We are creating a culture of community in our connection-driven classrooms, a supportive, respectful community. One where everyone feels safe to share and that they belong. When someone feels like they belong in the community, they want to take care of that community and defend that community, and that's the feeling we want to instill. We are not out to get each other; we are out to help each other. We're a team, which makes everyone's win a win for all of us. We're a team, which makes everyone's challenge a challenge we help solve. Small shifts occur. More students attend class. More students show up on time. More engagement happens in class discussions. More assignments get turned in at a higher quality. Test scores improve. Grades improve. More students go on to the next educational level.

And if the worst happens and a student leaves for a while, they are more likely to come back to a place they felt valued, seen, and heard.

A vicious cycle becomes a success cycle.

And if this feeling extends beyond just one classroom and educator to many, to administrators down through maintenance staff, then soon the whole school becomes the team, and everyone wants to treat each other better, take care of each other and their school spaces, and do better to live up to positive expectations.

The Connection-Driven Classroom can shift the whole feel of a school's climate to one of encouragement instead of discouragement. It can give everyone back their *why*.

But only if the whole school commits to a culture shift. One educator can only change one classroom—their group of students in that space. It takes the highest level of leadership, including the campus principal, to change the whole school, to shift what indicators and outcomes they want to focus on. They must give permission to their lower-level administrators to support the CDC, participate in it, and track it, and for their teachers and staff to practice it. If the CDC is not a priority at the top level, it will only be found in small oases in individual classrooms, practiced inconsistently and inefficiently. It will be hidden away in fear from school leaders because it's not "instructional" or focused on content and could be used as a reason for not meeting other goals like test scores.

The minute schools get stressed about mandated outcomes; relationships are the first thing that go out the door. The answer to better scores must be in those two extra minutes at the end of class, if we could just stuff more content in there. More pressure. More stress. But does this ever work? Do the numbers really improve when a class focuses solely on content and test prep? Where's the data on that?

The CDC works, but it works best if everyone gets into the pool with both feet. This is what we teach in our open-enrollment training to become a Certified Educator in Restorative Practices (CERP), at our annual conference, and in our formal school partnerships. Teachers need to proactively build community with the TCT tools in the classroom with their students, and school leaders need to respond relationally to correctional challenges that fall beyond a teacher's responsibility and scope. In this book, we have given educators the tools they need in the classroom based on our experience.

How will this help my students' academic performance?

The Wingspread Declaration on School Connections, issued in 2003, emphasized the critical role of fostering connections within schools to enhance students' academic performance and well-being. It outlined that students who feel a strong sense of belonging and connection to their school are more likely to succeed academically, engage in positive behaviors, and show reduced engagement in risky activities. The declaration highlighted the necessity of creating supportive, safe, and caring school environments where meaningful relationships between students and adults are prioritized. Recommendations were made for schools to implement practices that build these connections, recognizing the profound impact of adult-student relationships on students' overall development. Essentially, the declaration advocated for a holistic educational approach that values emotional well-being and community as integral to student success.[16]

So now we've reached the end of our time together. There is an African proverb: "the child who is not embraced by the village will burn it down to feel its warmth." We need to think of the village as encompassing everyone, from students to parents to teachers to staff. Yes, it even includes school administrators and leaders. I spent time on the administrative side; I should know.

School administrators, please hear me when I say this: If a campus principal wants to change the culture and cultivate a campus where connection-driven practices are the foundation of all other initiatives, then you MUST have two feet in this work. If you put one foot in and one foot out, you will experience minimal success.

Please don't assume or have staff members infer that if you brought an initiative in for professional learning, that means you automatically support it. The truth is, I have been on many campuses training staff, where the principal does not support this work. A higher power mandated it. If you are two feet in, I would encourage you to tell your staff, "This is my why for having us implement X, Y, Z, and I give you permission to go back to the class and use these strategies." There is that power in permission again.

Then, follow up your statement with your actions. When you get into those classrooms for an evaluation and observe your staff creating connections, jump in there! Shift from evaluate to participate. This action will reinforce to your staff that your why and actions are aligned.

Hopefully, this book convicted you at an uncertain time, when the extra stresses from a pandemic and other local and global threats and upheavals have left great cracks in an already strained

---

[16] https://files.eric.ed.gov/fulltext/ED511993.pdf

system. We're all stressed. We're all emotional. We all need grace, compassion and support. These things are much easier to manage, and much more sustainable to give, if we work in a connected community. A community that recognizes each other's humanity. A community that can forgive each other's mistakes and disagreements. That can recognize when we're struggling. When we're ordinary.

At one of our Houston talks, an educator approached me. Bluntly, she said, "If one person would've asked me one time if I was okay…but it never happened."

Like my cat, Kai, this educator was doing everything she could at her school to say, "Value me! See me! Hear me!" She was practically shouting, "I'm right *here*!"

And no one noticed.

But you are noticed now. If this book spoke your language, you've found your tribe.

If you can find one tool for one classroom, for just one student, our time together was worth it. I'll know I've done my job. That answers my why and the dream of a fourth-grade boy.

As I mentioned in the introduction, if these concepts light you up because they reflect your why, consider having your staff trained in the CDC, or if you want to build your capacity and train your staff in the CDC, check out our Trainer of Trainers program so you can continue inspiring teachers to connect. In addition, if you feel the theme of this book, "The Currency of Connections," would be a tremendously motivating message for your staff to hear, reach out to me to speak in your district or on your campus. Lastly, I do stand-up comedy for educators if you want to make your teachers laugh about our educational struggles.

Every child deserves and needs to have real connections with their educators. And this must happen before any curricular learning can be framed in any meaningful and sustainable way. So value, see, and hear connections. Build your school on the concrete of connections, not the sands of initiatives, through the intentional use of CDC and its TCT tools.

Everything comes out of relationships. And that means

everything. That means content, social-emotional intelligence, diversity, cultural awareness, the whole lot. Connections must come first. And they must be cultivated through small but regular touch points throughout the school year that ensure students and educators in one community are valued, seen, and heard.

This is what forms real cross-connections. This is what forms real relationships. Ones that last. Ones that are resilient. Ones that make it through the tough times and provide a base to rebuild initiatives and content when they get knocked down by personal and global events, we, as educators, can't control.

Connections help students succeed. Connections support outstanding educators. Connections create a new foundation to rebuild a broken system. So let's cultivate a learning environment where teachers can teach, students can learn, and leaders can lead.

Let's reimagine what a classroom can be.

So as you take a tool or two into your classroom to try something different, know that we value the work that you do. We see your struggle to find a better way. We hear what you've been asking for.

And here is our answer.

Acknowledgments

I want to express my deepest gratitude to everyone who has contributed to the creation of this book.

First and foremost, I would like to thank Denise "Circlemamma" Holliday. Your unwavering commitment to our friendship and our work, and your unique ability to remind me of the importance of love, have been invaluable. You have been my constant support and inspiration, standing by me even during the most challenging times. Your role in our circle of life is irreplaceable, and I love you more than words can express, sis, and there is nothing you can do about it.

I would also like to express my deep appreciation to my colleague and contributing author, Alan Krenek. Your creative thinking and passion have been instrumental in bringing this project to life. Your contributions to this book are a true gift, and I am proud to call you, my friend.

I would also like to thank Amanda Lemon for your time and commitment to helping me find the right words. Your editing and content creation skills were essential in giving this book the needed life. Amazing job, Amanda!

My heartfelt thanks also go to my peers and team at Differentiated Discipline. With your experiences, feedback, and support, this book exists. I am particularly grateful to Dr. Cassandra Darst, Dr. Jessica Moreno, Luke Schmidt, Tere Tidwell, Sandra Velo, and Judy Schiller for their editorial help, creation of graphics, keen insight, and ongoing support in bringing this dream to reality. I am forever indebted to all of you for always believing in me.

I would also like to thank the individuals who have played an integral role in contributing to this book, including Jerry Crowell,

Donald Bosier, Sarah Nunn, John Whalen, Doug Overton, Chris Riddick, Rufus Lott, Robert Rico, Eric Butler, Sherwynn Patton, Dr. Gaye Lange, Dr. Marilyn Armour, Stephanie Frogge, Phil Carney, Jackie Wade, and the students and staff of Ed White Middle School. Your support and contribution over the years is incalculable, and I am grateful for you all.

Finally, I want to express my gratitude to God, without whom none of this would be possible. Thank you for giving me the strength and inspiration to pursue this dream.

About the Author

Kevin W. Curtis is a powerhouse in the world of education. A visionary leader, he has dedicated his career to transforming how we think about school discipline and behavior management. As the founder of Differentiated Discipline, formerly National Educators for Restorative Practices (NEDRP), Kevin has established himself as a leading expert in connection-driven practices. He has a reputation for innovation, creativity, and results-driven strategies.

Kevin's groundbreaking work has been recognized nationwide, earning him a reputation as a sought-after speaker, comedian, and trainer. He has delivered keynote addresses and presentations at conferences and workshops nationwide, captivating audiences with his dynamic and engaging style. His passion for helping campuses cultivate their schools on the "concrete of connections" is palpable, and his deep expertise and wealth of knowledge have made him a transformational leader in the field.

Kevin's contributions to discipline and behavior are unparalleled. He is the coauthor of *Restorative Discipline Practices: A Journey in Implementation from a Community of Texas Educators,* a highly acclaimed guide to implementing restorative practices in schools. This book is a testament to Kevin's commitment to creating safe and supportive learning environments.

Kevin brings a unique and powerful blend of skills to the world of education. With over two decades of experience in K–12 public education, he is a master at creating engaging and transformative learning experiences. Kevin is a triple threat: he can train, perform standup comedy, and speak with authority.

Learn: Kevin's training sessions are packed with actionable insights and proven strategies for educators to foster stronger student connections and improve classroom dynamics.

Laugh: With his background in standup comedy, Kevin infuses humor into his presentations, making learning enjoyable and memorable. His comedic approach breaks down barriers and creates a relaxed environment conducive to effective learning.

Lead: As a captivating speaker, Kevin inspires educators to take charge and lead confidently. His messages of empowerment and practical advice equip teachers to become leaders in their schools and communities.

Through his work, Kevin is changing the landscape of education. He believes that every student deserves to feel valued, respected, and supported in their learning journey and that connection-driven practices are critical for achieving this goal. By prioritizing connections and fostering accountability, Kevin is helping to create a more just, equitable, and compassionate educational system that prioritizes students' needs.

For anyone looking to create a collaborative support system that cultivates connections and holds students accountable for their voices and choices, Kevin W. Curtis is the ultimate guide and mentor. His innovative strategies and unwavering commitment to student success make him an indispensable educational voice.

Scan to visit the LinkTree for Differentiated Discipline

Milton Keynes UK
Ingram Content Group UK Ltd.
UKHW022330271124
451619UK00014B/122/J

9 781964 014425